Term Limits in the State Legislatures

Term Limits
in the State Legislatures

John M. Carey
Richard G. Niemi
and
Lynda W. Powell

Ann Arbor

THE UNIVERSITY OF MICHIGAN PRESS

Copyright © by the University of Michigan 2000
All rights reserved
Published in the United States of America by
The University of Michigan Press
Manufactured in the United States of America
⊚ Printed on acid-free paper

2003   2002   2001   2000   4   3   2   1

A CIP catalog record for this book is available from the British Library.

Library of Congress Cataloging-in-Publication Data

Carey, John M.
    Term limits in the state legislatures / John M. Carey, Richard G. Niemi, and Lynda W. Powell.
        p.   cm.
    Includes bibliographical references and index.
    ISBN 0-472-09699-0 (cloth : alk. paper) — ISBN 0-472-06699-4 (pbk. : alk. paper)
    1. Legislators—Term of office—United States—States.   2. Term limits (Public office)—United States—States.   I. Niemi, Richard G. II. Powell, Lynda W.

JK2488 .C37   2000
328.73'073—dc21   00-023333

Contents

Tables

Acknowledgments

First and foremost, we thank the state legislators who contributed to our study. Thousands of state legislators filled out our mail questionnaire, and twenty-two legislators took time from their busy schedules to answer lengthy questions in person and by telephone. We are very grateful to all these individuals: without their help we could not have written this book.

We also thank the National Science Foundation (Grant SBR-9422375) for making it possible to conduct the survey and to carry out the research. The mail survey was carried out by the Polimetrics Lab at Ohio State University. We are grateful to the lab and its then director, Kathleen Carr. We also appreciate the help of the National Conference of State Legislatures, which provided the names and addresses of current and former legislators as well as a variety of information on legislatures and legislators.

Chris Collet at the University of California, Irvine, did the enormous job of updating the State Legislative Elections file for 1991 through 1994. Earlier data have for some time been available through the Inter-University Consortium for Political and Social Research. Amy Makinen and other graduate students at the University of Rochester helped us to create and keep track of files and to gather supplementary data.

The results in chapters 2, 3, and 4 were previewed in an article in *Legislative Studies Quarterly* (May 1998). However, none of the material from the personal interviews appears in that article. For comments and suggestions, we would like to thank the anonymous reviewers for the *Quarterly* and the University of Michigan Press, as well as discussants at various meetings at which we have presented parts of our findings.

CHAPTER 1

Ideas behind the Reform

Legislative term limits, the grassroots electoral reform that swept across much of the United States in the early 1990s, began to kick in during the latter half of the decade. Entire cohorts of lawmakers were removed from office, first in California and Maine; then in Arkansas, Colorado, Michigan, Montana, and Oregon; and subsequently in eleven other states. The onset of limits raises a number of questions about their effects. Among the most pressing: Do term limits produce a new breed of state legislator? Do they alter legislators' behavior and priorities? Do they affect the balance of power among the various actors in the legislative process? Do they affect competition in the broader political system beyond state legislatures? Our summary answers to these questions are as follows: (1) less than one might expect; (2) in some ways yes, in others no; (3) yes, indeed; and (4) yes, under specific conditions. Of course, such summaries inevitably raise more questions—of the who, how, when, and why variety—than they answer. Our purpose in this book is to take the broader questions apart, articulate their logic and their implications, and provide answers to the resulting specific questions about how term limits do (and do not) affect the composition of state legislatures, legislator behavior, various institutional actors' influence on policy, and the broader system of elections.

Debate on how term limits affect state legislatures was heated from the outset, as the reform was endorsed by voters in almost half of the states and, more recently, as legislatures and individual legislators confronted the reality of mandatory termination. The movement's high-water mark was 1992–94, when, in the course of just two years, seventeen states passed legislation or constitutional amendments limiting the length of time that state legislators could serve, and most of these states imposed limits on their congressional representatives as well. The first major setback came in 1995, when the Supreme Court declared limits on members of Congress to be unconstitutional.[1] The term-limits movement's momentum slowed further as it ran short of states in which citizen-initiated initiatives could launch ballot propositions and as subsequent court cases raised doubts about the legality of state legislative term limits. The considerable early successes of the movement were subject to delayed gratification, moreover, because most term-limit laws exempted service prior to the date when the legislation or amendment passed. Until 1996, therefore, no one was actually prohibited from reelection.

At the decade's end, interest in term limits, if not the reform movement itself, rebounded. California's state legislative term limits were upheld by the U.S. Circuit Court of Appeals, and the Supreme Court refused to hear an appeal.[2] Although term limits affected legislators in only California and Maine in 1996, by November 1998 more than two hundred incumbent legislators in seven states—including at least half of the Arkansas and Michigan lower houses—were ineligible to run (Chi and Leatherby 1998, 12), and limits are scheduled to go into effect in four more states in 2000. Though limits were overturned in three states (Massachusetts, Nebraska, and Washington),[3] limits are in place in eighteen states overall and, we anticipate, will be an established, regular part of the election process in all of these sites. The details of term-limits measures passed in the states are described in table 1.1.[4]

Despite sustained controversy over limits in the press, the courts, Congress and the state legislatures, and reform groups since the first ballot initiatives almost a decade ago, political scientists have only recently begun to weigh in with empirical studies that directly address the effects of term limits in the states. Most analyses of limits were, of necessity until 1996, based on extrapolations from pre–term limit electoral data or from data from quite different electoral contexts. Immediately after 1996, the first studies of elections and legislative performance in the term-limits era naturally focused only on California and Maine, the first two states in which incumbents were legally proscribed from office (see, e.g., Daniel and Lott 1997; Chi 1997). This book is the first study to assess the effects of term limits on state legislatures using survey data and election results from all fifty states as well as extensive interview data with legislators in four states. We present data from a 1995 nationwide survey of more than 3,000 current and former legislators. Given that by then nearly half of the states had adopted term limits, legislators and potential legislative candidates had begun anticipating limits' effects and adapting behavior accordingly.[5] Of course, behavior will continue to evolve, but some preliminary effects of term limits were already evident by the time of our survey. We also draw on electoral data from all state legislative elections from 1990–96 and on congressional elections in 1994 and 1996. The comprehensive survey and electoral data avoid problems of bias inherent in studies that focus on only a few states, particularly those studies that examine only states with limits. The comprehensive data also pointed toward subject matter that could be most profitably explored through subsequent in-depth interviews with legislators. Due to obvious time and cost constraints, we could not conduct such interviews with representative samples of legislators in all states. Instead, we drew on initial analysis of the survey data to guide follow-up interviews in 1997 with legislative party and committee leaders in four states—California, Maine, Massachusetts, and Washington—where term limits either had already taken effect or were pending.

The rest of this chapter consists of four sections. The first discusses the logic of reelection-based theories of legislative behavior and organization, extending them to establish some general expectations about the effects of term limits. The second briefly reviews and critiques the academic literature on term limits, establishing the relevance and contribution of our study. The third discusses our methodology for gathering survey and interview data on term limits and provides an introduction to the terminology we employ in discussing these data, focusing on the specific units of comparison we believe are relevant in analyzing the effects of term limits. The fourth section provides an overview of the chapters that follow.

Legislative Theory and Expectations about Term Limits

A central assumption in most legislative theory is that politicians are ambitious and that, as a consequence, legislative behavior and organization cannot be explained without paying close attention to political career opportunities and trajectories (Schlesinger 1966; Fenno 1978; Arnold 1990). Careerism is expected to affect the types of individuals who seek and win legislative seats, their behavior in office, and how they organize the legislatures in which they serve. This idea is more explicit in some accounts than others, but it is a linchpin of virtually all legislative theory. Thus, open critics of careerism attribute pork-barrel spending, excessive government regulation, and bureaucratic inefficiency to legislators' efforts to build constituency support (Fiorina 1989). The logical extension of this argument is that legislative careerism perpetuates a bias toward the recruitment and election to office of individuals whose backgrounds and philosophy predispose them to favor an intrusive, activist government (Ehrenhalt 1991; Will 1992). Moreover, even in work that, on the surface, appears further removed from the issue of careerism, like the ongoing debate over the relative importance of parties versus committees in legislative organization, the ultimate motivator of individual politicians is presumed to be the way that one's effort translates into district support for reelection (Cox and McCubbins 1993; Krehbiel 1992). In short, even within ongoing debates over how and to what effect power is distributed within legislatures, most theory actually takes as a starting point Mayhew's (1974, 81–82) conclusion regarding the U.S. Congress: "If a group of planners sat down and tried to design . . . assemblies with the goal of

TABLE 1.1. Term Limits on State Legislators

State	Lower House (years)[a]	Upper House (years)[a]	Year Adopted	Percent Support	Year of First Impact		Mechanism[b]	Break in Service[c]
					Lower House	Upper House		
Arizona	8	8	1992	74	2000	2000	S	2 years
Arkansas	6	8	1992	60	1998	2002	S	lifetime
California	6	8	1990	52	1996	1998	S	lifetime
Colorado	8	8	1990	71	1998	1998	S	4 years
Florida	8	8	1992	77	2000	2000	B	2 years
Idaho	8/15	8/15	1994	59	2002	2002	B	contingent
Louisiana	12	12	1995	76	2007	2007	S	4 years
Maine	8	8	1993	68	1996	1996	S	2 years
Massachusetts	8	8	1994	52	—[d]		B	2 years
Michigan	6	8	1992	59	1998	2002	S	lifetime
Missouri	8	8	1992	75	2002	2002	S	lifetime
Montana	8/16	8/16	1992	67	2000	1998	B	contingent
Nebraska	8[e]		1994	68	—[d]		S	2 years
Nevada	12	12	1994	70	2008	2008	S	lifetime
Ohio	8	8	1992	68	2000	2000	S	4 years
Oklahoma	12 years total in legislature		1990	67	2004	2004	S	lifetime
Oregon	6[f]	8[f]	1992	70	1998	2002	S	lifetime
South Dakota	8	8	1992	64	2000	2000	S	2 years
Utah	12	12	1994	—[g]	2006	2006	S	2 years
Washington	6/12[h]	8/14[h]	1992	52	—[d]		B	contingent
Wyoming	12/24	12/24	1992	77	2006	2006	S	contingent

Source: Limits, year adopted, and year of first impact are from Chi and Leatherby 1998 (corrected for Oregon lower house). Percent support is from National Conference of State Legislatures web site (http://www.ncsl.org/). Mechanism and break in service are from texts of state measures.

Note: States have varying provisions for counting partial terms due to appointment or special election. In many states, limits are defined in terms of times elected rather than years served or contain a clause such as "or, but for resignation, would have served."

[a] Number of years an individual may serve before term limits are applied. A pair of numbers indicates that an individual may not serve more than a certain number of years over a longer period—e.g., six of twelve years—whether or not those years are consecutive.

[b] Strict term limits (S) prohibit service in the legislature. Ballot access restrictions (B) prevent a candidate's name from being placed on the ballot but do not prevent a candidate from being elected on write-in votes.

[c] Length of time an individual must "sit out before serving (or having ballot access) again. The time may be contingent when the term limit law specifies that an individual may serve no more than a certain number of years over a longer period.

[d] Term limits were overturned by the courts in Massachusetts in 1997, in Nebraska in 1996, and in Washington in 1998.

[e] Nebraska's legislature is unicameral.

[f] No more than 12 years total in the legislature.

[g] Passed by the legislature in early 1994.

[h] No more than 14 out of 20 years combined in both houses of the legislature.

serving members' electoral needs year in and year out, they would be hard pressed to improve on what exists."

The most extensive exploration of the implications of ambition and careerism, of course, has focused on the U.S. Congress, which has long been sufficiently professionalized that it is feasible to build a political career within a single legislative chamber (Polsby 1968). Nevertheless, research on state legislatures shows that, especially over the past thirty years, professionalization and compensation have increased sufficiently that many state houses offer attractive venues in which ambitious politicians can build careers (Moncrief and Thompson 1992). Not surprisingly, reelection margins for incumbents and tenure levels have increased correspondingly (Breaux and Jewell 1992; Garand 1991; Weber, Tucker, and Brace 1991). If careerism accounts for who runs for and wins legislative office, how legislators behave, and how legislatures operate, then term limits present an enormous challenge to existing theory for the obvious reason that they legally proscribe building political careers within a legislative chamber.

We begin our study of term limits against this theoretical backdrop. It suggests a natural distinction among four areas in which term limits might be expected to have a measurable impact on legislatures: composition, behavior, institutions, and the broader electoral arena. The first concerns the types of individuals who seek and win office; the second concerns their priorities and activities in office; the third concerns the manner in which power is distributed within legislatures and between legislatures and other policymakers; and the fourth concerns the level of competition for other elected offices, as ambitious politicians banished from their state legislative chambers turn their attention to alternative political prizes. In subsequent chapters, we establish in detail our specific measurements of compositional, behavioral, institutional, and broader electoral effects of term limits. At this point, we merely point to a general expectation we think derives from ambition-based legislative theories and foreshadow our conclusions.

The initial expectation is that, with respect to the state legislatures themselves, the effects of term limits should be felt sequentially in composition, behavior, and institutions because, in all the states in which they have been adopted, term limits were put on the books well before they actually began forcing legislators out of office. As early as 1990 in California, Colorado, and Oklahoma, in 1992 in eleven other states, and by 1994 in six more (not including Nebraska), term limits became law, meaning that legislators in office knew the specific date at which their service would end, and prospective legislators knew the maximum term they could serve. Consider what this development means for our various areas of expected term-limit effects. Legislative institutions represent the collective organizational decisions of large groups and tend to be relatively stable over time. One might expect that, if term limits are to trigger significant institutional changes, entire new cohorts of politicians must first be elected under the term-limits regime. It is also reasonable to think that legislative behavior is shaped both by career ambition and by the institutional context within which a politician serves. Thus, although we expect some behavioral changes early on after the adoption of term limits, these expectations are modest. If term limits are to affect the composition of legislatures, however, there is every reason to believe that these effects should show up immediately. Once term limits are the law of the land, any effects on who decides to run for office and how to allocate campaign resources should be evident in the composition of all subsequent legislative cohorts. Compositional effects might filter through to stimulate behavioral and institutional effects in time, but composition might be expected to be the first of our three areas to show measurable effects as the result of term limits.

Our empirical conclusions, in fact, are precisely the reverse. Term limits had remarkably little initial effect on the demographics and ideology of those elected to state legislatures. Effects on legislative behavior and institutions, however, were already apparent even before term limits legally prevented their first legislator from returning to office. True to the claims of many term-limits adherents, the reforms appear to inhibit the sorts of district-oriented activities and priorities among legislators that are generally associated with pure electioneering. At the same time, however, there is evidence that term limits are already weakening state legislatures relative to other actors in the policy-making process, as feared by reform opponents. We present the methods and evidence by which we reach these conclusions at length in subsequent chapters. First, it is worthwhile to review the existing literature on term limits to demonstrate how our study builds on existing knowledge.

Approaches to the Study of Term Limits

Initially, much of the debate over legislative term limits focused on the U.S. Congress. During the early 1990s, when outrage over high rates of reelection for congressional incumbents was at its peak, twenty-three states passed limitations on congressional reelection.[6] With a few long-standing members, such as Dan Rostenkowski and Tom Foley, providing high-profile targets for criticism, congressional term limits became a cause célèbre for political reformers. Academic debate over term limits largely followed suit, and most studies focused on how term limits would affect Congress. This particular line of debate was foreshortened in May 1995, when the Supreme Court, in *U.S. Term Limits, Inc. v. Thornton* (115 S.Ct. 1842), ruled that state-level limitations on congressional reelection violate the Qualifications Clauses of the Constitution (article 1, sections 2 and 3) and so are void. Despite support from Republican leaders, proposed constitutional amendments limiting reelection stalled in 1995 and 1996. Thus, in the wake of the Supreme Court decision, the term-limits debate appears most immediately relevant to state legislatures.[7]

Academic analysis of how term limits will affect legislatures has taken three main approaches. One has been to estimate how many members of a particular legislature have served long enough to be forced out of office under a particular term-limits plan (Moncrief et al. 1992; Everson 1992; Opheim 1994). This literature argues that the more legislators are forced to retire because of term limits rather than leaving voluntarily, the greater the impact of limits on the legislature. Such a conclusion, of course, is premised on the belief that legislators who replace those who are forced out will behave differently from their predecessors. This idea has been supported by studies of the U.S. Congress that find junior members to be less productive in passing legislation than are their senior counterparts (Hibbing 1991; Ahuja and Moore 1992). Of course, in the absence of any very senior members, junior members may themselves have greater opportunities for legislative entrepreneurship and may behave differently.

A second approach has been to distinguish between retiring and nonretiring legislators rather than between senior and junior legislators. The premise here is that term limits should change the degree to which legislators are responsive to their current constituents once they are certain not to be judged in the voting booth. Studies have found that attendance at congressional roll call votes declines among retiring members (Lott 1990; McArthur 1990) and that retirees alter their voting behavior slightly relative to their previous records (Zupan 1990; Carey 1994), though they do not violate the interests of their constituents as estimated by district demographics (Dougan and Munger 1989; Lott and Reed 1989). Another study found that retiring members are less active in introducing legislation and traveling to their districts and that they are more specialized and focused in pursuing their legislative agenda (Herrick, Moore, and Hibbing 1994). Of course, many retirees are older members ending not only their legislative careers but also their full-time employment. Younger members with an eye to a further career may behave differently from these individuals.

A third approach to the term-limit debate has been historical and comparative. The absence of recent experience with term limits in the United States has directed attention to the founding era, when term limits were tried briefly and unsuccessfully under the Articles of Confederation and debated at the Constitutional Convention of 1787 (Petracca 1992b). Others have turned to the experience of the handful of other countries that have imposed legislative term limits in an effort to trace their effects on political careers and legislative behavior (Carey 1996; Weldon 1994; Mejía Acosta 1996).[8] Although these studies may provide useful hypotheses and insights, the different political, electoral, and historical contexts pose serious problems for simple generalization to contemporary U.S. legislatures.

All these studies of term limits have serious shortcomings. The overwhelming attention given to Congress in the initial work was understandable, given the importance of the institution and the relative ease of collecting data. But with congressional term limits currently in limbo and state-level limits in place and taking effect, it is imperative to focus on state legislatures. In short, the first advantage of this study is that it directly examines the effects of term limits on the key population of interest—state legislators. Further, we regard this shift as a methodological opportunity rather than a burden. With ninety-nine legislative chambers, the states provide a natural laboratory for comparative analysis of the impact of term limits. Diversity across states allows us to control for the size and professionalism of legislatures as well as for the demographics of constituents when evaluating the effects of limits.

Previous approaches have other problems that this project also addresses. Earlier studies represent efforts to sidestep the fact that data on the effects of term limits in the United States have been nonexistent until quite recently. Though imaginative and ingenious at times, the first two approaches cannot avoid serious problems inherent in the samples of legislators they examine. Hypothetically removing all legislators who have served longer than term limits would permit, for example, assumes that the behavior of legislators who have served for less than that period would be unaffected by the existence of term limits. A fundamental premise at the heart of the term limits debate, however, is that prohibiting reelection should affect the behavior of incumbent legislators. Thus, simply distinguishing between senior and junior legislators ignores a critical issue.

The second approach, examining the behavior of legislators who have decided not to seek reelection, tries to remedy this problem by evaluating whether and how the behavior of legislators who are subject to the reelection constraint differs from those who are not. Empirical work along these lines rests on the assumption that the behavior of legislators who retire voluntarily can tell us something about the behavior of those who would be forced out of office by term limits. The problem is that legislators who are forced out of office by term limits are more likely to retain political career ambitions than are retirers. This intuition is supported by Herrick and Nixon's (1994) finding that U.S. House members who left office involuntarily (via an election loss or redistricting) were twice as likely to move immediately into lobbying jobs or political appointments as those who chose to leave the House. Carey (1994) addresses the behavior of retiring legislators who remain politically ambitious by examining the behavior of those who leave the House to run for statewide office, finding that such legislators alter their voting to accommodate their future constituencies. Yet this approach allows for the analysis of such a small sample of legislators that results must be interpreted cautiously.

Perhaps more importantly, neither of these approaches addresses the question of whether legislators elected under a term-limits regime would differ systematically from those elected in the absence of limits. This idea—that term limits should affect the composition of legislatures by altering the incentive to run—is generally taken as an article of faith by adherents and opponents of limits alike, yet it has never been systematically examined. By the time of our survey and interviews, term limits had been established in many states for at least two election cycles. Thus, if a term-limits regime has a measurable impact on the type of person who runs for and wins office, the differences ought to be apparent among legislators who were first elected after the adoption of term limits in their states. Whether term limits have any such effect is the central question addressed in chapter 2.

Finally, historical and comparative approaches represent efforts to avoid the problems inherent in the first two approaches. They allow for the direct examination of the behavior of ambitious politicians for whom the electoral connection has been severed, demonstrating that such politicians systematically seek patronage positions (Carey 1996; Weldon 1994). In trying to extend their conclusions to the current U.S. term-limits debate, however, such approaches run up against the question of the comparability of units. Only at a very general level can conclusions from political environments such as Costa Rica, Mexico, or Ecuador be extended to the United States. Likewise, the nature of political careers and legislative organization under the Articles of Confederation are sufficiently removed from the current context that their relevance is approximate at best. Moreover, historical work has tended to romanticize the politics of previous eras, offering paeans to the practice of rotation in office that ignore the connection between this practice and the construction of machine politics and the spoils system (Petracca 1992b; Will 1992). Thus, although comparative and historical methods provide valuable perspectives on the issue of term limits, we can learn about the effects of limits on U.S. state legislatures most precisely by directly studying the population of interest.

Data and Methodology

The 1995 Survey

The academic literature has taken the indirect approaches outlined previously because data on the effects of term limits in this country have been unavailable. In contrast, we undertook a survey that allows us to begin to examine directly the effects of state-level limits. As the first legislators were not prevented by term limits from running until a year after our survey was administered, it remains impossible to evaluate the full impact of term limits. Yet initial evidence of many important effects on state legislators was reported before term limits kicked in. Anecdotal reports on individual legislatures suggest that these effects were significant and immediate. Schrag (1995, 25), for example, decries the "12 special elections—that's 10 percent of all seats" in California, costing more than ten million dollars, that occurred between the regular 1992 and 1994 elections. Conversely, Holt (1996, 1) claims that Oregon legislators "are becoming increasingly agenda-oriented."[9] Our survey addressed a range of issues on which anticipatory effects of term limits could have been expected.

If term limits are systematically changing the composition of state legislatures by altering the pool of candidates who run for office, we should be able to detect these effects by comparing legislators first elected after the adoption of term limits in their states with those elected before that time. Moreover, because many of the legislators in our survey faced dates at which they were prohibited from seeking reelection, we should be able to determine whether term limits systematically alter the behavior of elected legislators once in office. Finally, we should be able to gain some preliminary indications of whether and how term limits affect the organization and strength of state legislatures at the aggregate level based on respondent perceptions of these issues. In short, our survey allows us to study the effects of term limits on state legislatures in a way that has previously been impossible.

Our survey was conducted in the spring of 1995. We mailed surveys to every member of the upper houses (including the single chamber in Nebraska) and to roughly three-quarters of the members of the lower houses in all fifty states.[10] In addition, we surveyed all former legislators who last served in 1993 or 1994 for whom National Conference of State Legislatures had valid addresses. The data are weighted here both to correct for the differential probability of selection in the lower chambers and to correct for differential response rates.[11] With the weights, the sample is representative of the population of all state legislators, where each legislator is counted equally. From the perspective employed in this work, this weighting is exactly as it should be, inasmuch as each state contributes to the sample in proportion to the size of its legislature. We shall, of course, control for chamber size in all multivariate analyses.

The 1997 Interviews

Almost two years after the surveys were administered, during the winter and spring of 1997, we conducted interviews with legislators in four states: Maine and California, where term limits had already proscribed reelection for the most senior legislators, as well as Washington and Massachusetts, where they were pending in two and four years, respectively. Whereas with the survey we aimed at collecting data on state legislators nationwide, the costs of conducting in-depth interviews required us to take a different approach with the interviews. Rather than aim at a comprehensive and unbiased sample of legislators, we focused our attention where we expected the effects of term limits to be most dramatic—where limits had already kicked in or were scheduled to do so shortly.

Within each legislature as well, we did not aim for a sample of legislators representative of the entire distribution. Rather, we sought interviews with those who held leadership positions within their parties and with committee chairs. We followed this strategy for a combination of practical and methodological reasons. On a practical level, we did not have the time or resources to contact and interview samples of legislators large enough to approximate the entire membership of any chamber. Methodologically, we had achieved such unbiased samples in our survey, and our intent with the interviews was different. We sought access to those senior legislators whom we regarded as best positioned to evaluate the impact of term limits on the phenomena of greatest interest to us: candidate recruitment, legislator priorities and commitments, committee organization and performance, party cohesiveness and discipline, and so forth. Thus, we do not intend interview results precisely to mirror those of the survey but rather to amplify them and, in so doing, to throw light on the mechanics behind the survey results.

That said, we did select our four interview states so that we drew legislatures from diverse geographical regions and so that the four states span the range of professionalization levels, from the most highly professionalized legislature in the country (California) to one of the least (Maine), with Massachusetts and Washington falling roughly along the quartiles in the distribution of professionalization.[12]

The time that elapsed between administration of the survey and the interviews allowed us to gather, clean, and analyze the massive survey data, so that interview questions could be designed to follow up on the most promising themes from the survey and to probe for explanations behind noteworthy and surprising results. Because the clock on term limits was ticking during the two crucial years between the survey and interviews, however, the environment in which the interviews were conducted differed from that of the survey in important ways. One should expect that the effects of term limits picked up in the interviews are more dramatic than in the surveys, because limits had already removed their first cohort of legislators from office in two of our interview states and were two years closer to taking effect in the others. This difference in the magnitude of effects is, indeed, notable in the interviews; however, equally remarkable is the overall consistency between survey and interview results in the substance of effects noted.

When reporting on our interview results, we generally do not count responses and report frequencies for a number of reasons. First, the number of interview subjects was too small to place much confidence in the distribution of responses. Second, because of legislators' time constraints during interviews, it was not always possible to ask every subject every question in the battery. Third, it is not always feasible to code open-ended interview responses as necessary to report distributions. Fourth, given the bias in our sample of interviewees toward senior legislators in party and committee leadership positions, we do not expect the results to be entirely reflective of the broader cross section of legislators. Finally, our purpose in the interviews was to elicit detailed comments from experienced legislators that could shed light on the survey data and suggest areas in which the concerns of the survey—and perhaps the larger debate surrounding term limits—should be redirected.

Method of Comparison

To assess the effects (or noneffects) of term limits, it is not enough to compare legislators in term-limit (TL) states and those in non-term-limit (NTL) states, as important as those comparisons are. As is true of all analyses in which one attempts to go beyond mere description, we must be concerned about the possible influence of other factors. Consider an example. State legislatures differ substantially by size (even setting aside New Hampshire, with its four-hundred-member lower house), and it is reasonable to suppose that the size of the legislature has something to do with the kinds of people who run for it and especially the way it operates. If most TL states had small legislatures and most NTL states had large legislatures, observed differences between legislators or legislative operations in TL and NTL states might have more to do with legislative size than with the existence of term limits.

The way to deal with this problem is through one form or another of statistical analysis, specifically, imposing controls on the analysis so that one can be relatively certain that the additional factors do not account for the difference in which one is interested. Thus, for example, if we compared only large TL and large NTL chambers and small TL and small NTL chambers, and the differences between TL and NTL states remained, we could be relatively certain that the original differences were not a product of chamber size.

It is also important throughout most of our analysis that we distinguish, within term-limit states, between legislators elected before and legislators first elected after term limits were adopted. We dub these groups old-timers (OTs) and newcomers (NCs), respectively. Incumbents first elected before term limits were adopted made their initial commitment to seek legislative office under a different set of rules, in a different political environment: by the mid-1990s, they had already established a pattern of legislative behavior and made whatever business, personal, and family adjustments were necessary to accommodate service in legislative office.[13] In contrast, those elected after the adoption of term limits made their decisions to run for the legislature knowing the specific limitations on their term of office. Although they may not have understood fully all the implications of term limits for the political system, they certainly would have taken into account the clear implications for the length of their legislative careers. Some potential candidates would have decided not to run, and thus the pool of candidates was shaped by expectations regarding the effects of term limits. Once elected, the legislative views, priorities, and styles of the new legislators in term-limited states were shaped by the constraints and opportunities of term limits.

Given the probable effects of time of first entry, legislators elected after the adoption of term limits must be compared with an identical group unaffected by term limits. The best comparison group consists of other legislators who were first elected recently but who are in states that did not adopt term limits. Matching the time period takes into account the fact that the political climate in the mid-1990s was quite different from that faced by members first elected in the 1970s and 1980s—more pro-Republican and markedly more hostile to incumbents. These characteristics presumably affected the types of candidates who chose to run and who succeeded, an area separate from the impact of term limits.

Accordingly, we distinguish between legislative newcomers and old-timers in term-limit and non-term-limit states. Newcomers were elected to the state legislature for the first time after term limits had been adopted in their states or, in the case of non-term-limit states, after 1992 (i.e., mostly in 1994 but a few in 1993 due to off-off-year elections). We made the cut-off point for non-term-limit states just after the 1992 elections because it was in that year that term-limit initiatives passed in the most states and the term-limit movement gained attention and momentum as a national issue. In all states, first-time candidates running after 1992 had to be aware that their newly intended careers might be even more precarious than is usual for elected offices.

Thus, using the two dichotomies, the one distinguishing between states by whether they had adopted term limits and the other distinguishing legislators by when they were elected, we identify four separate sets of legislators, whom we will often denote by their letter abbreviations:

OTNTLs: first elected to the legislature in 1992 or before in states that have not adopted term limits;

OTTLs: first elected to the legislature in or before the year in which term limits were adopted in their states;

NCNTLs: first elected to the legislature in 1993 or later in states that have not adopted term limits;

NCTLs: first elected to the legislature after term limits were adopted in their states.

Of course, this breakdown can be aggregated into NCs versus OTs or TL versus NTL states. Which subsets form the appropriate comparison groups depends on the question we are asking. We shall make this point clear as we present the results.

The world is not so simple, of course, that we can control for just this one factor—time of entry in the legislature. A variety of other factors might also affect comparisons between legislators in TL and NTL states, resulting in observed differences that do not really result from the imposition of term limits. Were we to ignore these other factors, we again run the risk of overstating the effects of term limits.

The most important of these additional controls is the professionalization of the legislature in which an individual serves. Professionalized legislatures attract individuals with specific qualities and generate specific sorts of behaviors that correspond directly to so many of the concerns underlying the term-limit movement that an analysis of term limits would be of little value without accounting for this factor. Therefore, following what has become standard practice, we created a measure of professionalization by combining data on legislative compensation, days in session, and expenditures for staff and other purposes.[14]

In addition to professionalization, we control for a host of other variables that could plausibly affect the composition and behavior of legislators and the organization of legislatures independently of term limits. Characteristics of legislative chambers include upper/lower house status, number of members, and number of constituents in each district. Characteristics of legislators themselves include their party affiliation and whether their party is in the majority in the legislative chamber.

Drawing on census data compiled by Lilley, DeFranco, and Diefenderfer (1994), we also control for demographic characteristics of the constituency, including income and education levels; proportion that is elderly; relative shares of farm, service industry, and government employment; and shares of Hispanic, Asian, black, and other populations. Controlling for type of constituency is especially important when we treat topics such as legislator-constituent relations or when we make any calculations relating to reelection possibilities.

Drawing on our survey, we also use the legislator's own estimate of the mix of partisan affiliations in the district and of district competitiveness. Finally, we typically include a dummy variable for the South. In a few instances, additional control variables are included; for example, in predicting family income of the legislator, age of the legislator is included. These variables will be mentioned in each specific case.

All these controls allow us much more precision in identifying the effects of term limits. Most importantly, they allow us to be reasonably confident that whatever differences we find among our subgroups of legislators are in fact driven by the existence or nonexistence of term limits and the legislators' status as old-timers or newcomers. Of course, such added confidence does not come without a price. The price is in the form of greater complexity—specifically, in the use of multivariate regression analysis as opposed to simple percentage differences. We shall attempt to overcome the requisite complexity in a variety of ways—by presenting the estimated effects of term limits separately from and more prominently than those of the control variables, by verbal interpretations of the statistical results, and by presenting summary tables at the end of each chapter that describe the measured effects of term limits without statistical notation. The tables that present statistical analyses will always include the detailed results for those willing and able to follow the analysis. Readers who lack the time or specialized skills needed to follow these details nonetheless have the assurance that, insofar as possible, we have isolated the effects of term limits, free of contamination from the many other factors that contribute to differences among state legislators and legislative chambers.

Plan of the Book

Subsequent chapters evaluate whether the expectations of term-limit advocates and opponents are borne out in four areas. Chapter 2 examines the effects of term limits on the composition of state legislatures—that is, whether the existence of limits has affected the demographic background of legislators and the nature of state legislative campaigns. Chapter 3 addresses the issue of legislative behavior, evaluating whether term limits alter the relationship between representatives and their constituents and the directions in which legislators channel their political efforts. Chapter 4 turns to the effects of term limits on legislative institutions, particularly the relative strength of party leadership, committee chairs, staff, lobbyists, and the executive branch. Chapter 5 shifts the focus to the effects of state legislative term limits throughout the political system, particularly to the potential for a trickle-up effect on competitiveness in upper chambers of the state legislature and on congressional elections. Chapter 6 sums up our results and offers general conclusions.

CHAPTER 2

Term Limits and the Composition of State Legislatures

There is consensus among term-limit supporters that legislatures—at both the state and congressional levels—have been performing inadequately and that new personnel are needed in legislative office. Beyond this initial agreement stand various explanations for legislative malaise and for the appropriate response. For some, the problem is simply careerism, whereby legislators remain in office for long periods of time. Increase turnover and the problem will be solved. For other critics, however, we need new kinds of legislators, not merely new legislators. The argument here is that reform must encourage the election of individuals who are less interested in their own careers and more interested in service to the state or nation and in legislative accomplishment.

Both perspectives come together in support for the term-limit movement. There are widely shared expectations that term limits will generate greater turnover and that increased turnover will change the characteristics of legislative candidates and of legislators. Minimally, proponents as well as opponents would agree, limiting the length of legislative service should reduce the attractiveness of the office to individuals seeking to make a career out of politics, thereby creating more opportunities for non-career-oriented individuals to serve in the legislature. Reformers expect this to end "politics as usual," opening up legislative office to persons without conventional political backgrounds—in particular to those who are not in the legal profession or prior holders of public office (Petracca 1991). Others suggest more generally that term limits will attract citizens of more diverse backgrounds to state legislative office (e.g., Fund 1992).

Expectations of change do not stop there. It is plausible that term limits could affect the issue positions and ideology of legislators. Ehrenhalt (1991) argues, for example, that liberals find government careers inherently more attractive than do conservatives because of beliefs about the place of government in society. Reforms that discourage careers in politics thus may make political institutions attractive to a larger number of conservatives, who would be willing to make a short-term commitment to serve. One might also argue that reforms that reduce the social and material benefits of service would place greater reliance on the policy motivation for holding office, which could result in more strong ideologues running for and holding political office (Brown, Powell, and Wilcox 1995, chap. 4).

If term limits affect who runs for office and on what motivation, it is plausible that changes would show up in the nature of legislative campaigns and elections. First, term limits should increase turnover, not just as long-term legislators are legally prohibited from running for reelection but even earlier, as some incumbents leave preemptively to pursue other opportunities.[1] If changes in turnover and retirement rates are unequal across parties, then term limits can be expected to affect the partisan composition of legislatures. Many Democrats certainly suspected that widespread Republican support for the reforms in the early 1990s was driven by the fact that there were far more Democratic than Republican incumbents in both state legislatures and Congress. Moreover, statistical models based not only on raw numbers of incumbents but also on the rate at which incumbents successfully defended seats and at which parties divided open seats during the 1970s and 1980s, predicted Republican gains at the congressional level under term limits (Gilmour and Rothstein 1994). Conversely, the massive gains made by Republicans in 1994, before term limits took effect, could change this calculus considerably.

At the individual level, the schedule of vacancies in legislative seats imposed by term limits might affect decisions by prospective candidates on whether and when to run, which in turn could affect the competitiveness of elections. Effects on competitiveness and on the value of legislative office, moreover, could affect the effort and resources expended by candidates. If the value of state legislative office declines, campaigns could become less costly and less professional (Mitchell 1991; Daniel and Lott 1997). Alternatively, term limits could increase the professionalization of campaigns in two ways. First, more nonincumbents would be running for the legislature, and open-seat races tend to be competitive relative to those with an incumbent running for reelection. Second, incumbents who aspire to other posts (e.g., state senate seats or statewide office) might make efforts to expand their campaign resources and organization. With accurate and comprehensive data on campaign finance across all states unavailable, we evaluate effects on campaigns by examining the rates at which candidates hire campaign managers and establish campaign headquarters as well as the frequency with which challengers defeat incumbent legislators.

With respect to demographics and ideology, the primary question is whether the newcomers in term limit states (NCTLs) differ systematically from newcomers in non-term-limit states (NCNTLs). As noted in chapter 1, a straightforward comparison of these two groups will be misleading if there are systematic differences between term-limit and non-term-limit states apart from limits themselves; thus, the analysis must be somewhat more sophisticated if we wish to attribute observed differences to term limits. Our solution is to include both old-timers and newcomers, along with the control variables discussed in the previous chapter, in statistical analyses. Doing so allows us to compare each of three groups—old-timers in term-limit states along with the two sets of newcomers—to OTNTLs, which for our purposes, may be regarded as archetypal legislators uncontaminated by the term-limits movement. If OTTLs do not differ systematically from OTNTLs, then we can conclude that any difference between the two newcomer groups is not driven by inherent differences between term-limit and non-term-limit states, and we are therefore much more confident that it is the product of term limits themselves. However, if there is a significant difference between old-timers from term-limit and non-term-limit states, it tells us that even legislators elected before 1993 differed systematically across these states. In this case, the results are difficult to interpret; they may represent inherent differences between term-limit and non-term-limit states, or they may be attributable to differential effects of term limits on more senior legislators in term-limit states.

Demographics

One of the rallying cries of those who support term limits is that they will bring "new blood" and new ideas to state legislatures. Term limits will almost certainly reduce the overall level of legislative experience, simply by preventing extended careers within a specific chamber. Although opinion is sharply divided over whether shorter careers improve the quality of representation, even those otherwise opposed to limits concede that cleaning house may encourage policy change by altering the composition of legislatures. According to our lone interview respondent who requested anonymity,

> We really do need some new blood in here. I spent some years on the Committee on Education, and you had some guys who had been there for twenty, thirty years who had no interest in innovation or trying anything new. I mean, they just basically were defenders of the status quo—and they were Democrats. And I was a Democrat pushing for innovation, and they didn't want to hear anything. And it was very frustrating. A bunch of octogenarians who will never have another child in the schools were trying to tell me that I don't know what's right for kids.

Such a statement begs the question of whether term limits have any systematic impact on who runs for and serves in state legislatures. As it turns out, despite all the speculation about term limits producing a new breed of legislator, our results show no clear change in composition that can be attributed to the reform.

Noneffects of Term Limits: Recruitment, Occupation, Age, Education, Income, Religion

Legislators themselves gave a mixed report on the presumed effects of term limits on the recruitment of candidates, whether in general or when talking specifically about possible changes in demographics. There was some expectation of change, but even those who talked of such a possibility saw it as being limited in nature. According to Senator Brian Lees (R-MA),

> I don't know if [there will be] a different type of individual, but I think you'll see more people running for office, because term limits will make it easier for new people to get involved because you won't have people entrenched for all that period of time. I mean, it will turn around individuals and it will give some people that maybe in the past wouldn't have run against somebody if they happened to be in the district with someone who was middle-aged, that was very entrenched, that was going to be there for thirty or forty years, the opportunity to run.

Although term limits had been on the books for more than six, four, three, and two years, respectively, in the states in which we interviewed, those legislators who expected term limits to affect recruitment saw it as a future possibility but not a current reality. Democrat Thomas Finneran, the Speaker of the Massachusetts House, said,

> This is prospective, downstream, because it hasn't kicked in here in Massachusetts. I think that the political arena is something that tends to deny, or not absolutely react to, something that is prospective, or out in the future. You begin to see the more immediate results of this when in fact it kicks in.

Contrary to the conventional assumption that politicians are perpetually strategic and decide when and for what office to run based on expectations about career prospects (Schlesinger 1966; Jacobson and Kernell 1981), the interviews leave the general impression that legislators and potential candidates make short-term calculations.

In addition, some of our interview respondents thought that term limits would make it more difficult to convince quality candidates to run. Finneran sums up this perspective:

> While you might be able to draw from a larger pool, it's discouraging to anybody to think that no matter how hard they work, no matter how successful they prove to be, or how skilled they are, there is this iron curtain that falls down. And it falls down on the good and bad alike. I think that would be terribly unsettling to those people who may be being recruited on the basis of merit. You're obviously going to be picking people who are talented or energetic, who have a work ethic—that's what would draw me to them in the first place. And then to tell that person, again, no matter how well they labor in the vineyard, their career is a short career . . .

The same sentiment was echoed in a far less professionalized legislature, where meager compensation means that even lengthy service by itself could hardly provide a career. According to Democrat Mark Lawrence, the Senate majority leader in Maine, where term limits were already in operation at the time of the interview,

> It is much more difficult to recruit candidates at this point. It's always difficult to recruit candidates, but because we have a citizen legislature and there are so many sacrifices you have to make to serve, it's always difficult, and term limits have made it increasingly challenging to go out and find candidates.

In the case of less-professionalized legislatures, there is another consideration. Constraints on who can serve that are unrelated to term limits may simply swamp any effects of the reform. Interview subjects in Maine were quick to place term limits in such a context. Said Democrat Joseph Mayo,

> We tend to have people, because we're a citizen legislature, in two groups: the young and inexperienced and the older and retired. People who don't have a lot of time demands and don't have a lot of family concerns and monetary concerns can come serve as a legislator, so we have a large number of individuals who are relatively young. . . . And we tend to have people who are along in their careers and have the security they need in order to take time off to come here. So, that hasn't changed. Term limits, I don't believe, will affect that.

Dan Gwadosky, a Democrat, pointed out,

We do keep track generally of occupation and sometimes income and sometimes whether they're single or have a family and those types of things. We haven't seen a lot [of] difference. Our pay in Maine is still relatively low, [so] that the pay itself in the session schedule is a bigger determination as to who will serve or not. . . . So a lot of people just can't afford to take that amount of time off to serve and so by nature of that we've had a lot of retirees, we've had a lot of women, and that's been an encouraging sign. We've always been in the top five or top ten in the country in terms of women participation and women in leadership roles certainly, too. That's been dramatic—this year more than ever. I think that the pay itself and the length of the session are bigger in determining who serves in any one session or who runs than term limits, at least to date.

Our survey data are consistent with the sentiments expressed in the interviews. Few if any changes in demographic representation occurred in the immediate aftermath of the adoption of term limits. Consider, for example, occupation. We coded our respondents' jobs prior to legislative service into ninety-eight categories and selected the three most common— lawyer, insurance agent, and real estate agent—to determine whether these occupations are any more or less common among post–term limit legislators. They are not. There is no significant difference between NCTLs and NCNTLs, or between the old-timers in the two types of states, in the proportion of legislators drawn from these professions.

It is possible, of course, that term limits could affect the relationship between occupation and legislative representation without altering the distribution of occupational backgrounds across legislators. Senator Dede Alpert (D-CA), for example, articulates the concern that professions with well-organized interest groups will send delegates whose careers remain tied more closely to their profession than to the legislature and whose behavior is correspondingly affected:

> *Alpert:* One of my concerns is that maybe certain special-interest groups will decide to run a teacher or a nurse—the list kind of goes on and on—get someone within their profession to be willing to do it for six years, so that you may see more and more people who are really oriented toward one issue running for the legislature.
> *Interviewer:* Have you seen specific examples of that?
> *Alpert:* Yes, I think we are just beginning to see that as we see the newest members. . . . That's what some groups figure: "Heck, if it is just for six years, we'll send one of our teachers, or one of our

nurses up, and then they can represent our interest inside the legislature."

We need more extended analyses of legislative processes and policy outcomes and comparisons of the pre- and postlegislative career paths of
politicians before Alpert's suggestion can be confirmed or rejected. The
most striking aspect of our initial results, however, is the lack of impact of
term limits on the demographic characteristics we can measure.

Apart from occupation, race, religion, age, education, and income are
key demographic indicators that show no evidence of any effect. There is
no difference in the average level of education or family income of legislators across any of our four groups of legislators or in the likelihood that a
legislator is black or a fundamentalist Christian. In short, once we control
for the demographics of state legislative districts and the characteristics of
the legislatures themselves, we find no systematic differences in the backgrounds of legislators from term-limit and non-term-limit states, whether
we are talking about old-timers or newcomers.

Representation of Women

The representation of women in the state legislatures deserves special
attention. Despite continued underrepresentation in terms of their proportion in the population, the percentage of women has grown substantially in recent years (Norrander and Wilcox 1998). Term limits, in spite of
their general noneffects on demographic representation, may have contributed to this recent growth in the number of women. It is particularly
important to look at the representation of women because the coincidence
of the term-limits movement and the rise in representation of women
might instead mislead one into thinking that the two are causally related
when in fact they are related only temporally. Indeed, former Representative Gwadosky of Maine, quoted earlier, suggested that high levels of representation for women in his state are attributable to the nonprofessional-
ized nature of the legislature rather than to term limits.

As it turns out, gender is the only background characteristic on which
we find statistically significant differences between term-limit and non-
term-limit states. Yet even here, on close examination the data do not tell
a straightforward story of term limits encouraging the election of more
women. First, there is a simple difference across states. Table 2.1 shows the
percentage of women among each of our four groups of legislators,
OTNTLs, OTTLs, NCNTLs, and NCTLs, with the marginal values showing the aggregate percentage across cohorts and in term-limit and non-
term-limit states. While the difference is not large, it is apparent that states

with term limits elected more women to their state legislatures in 1995 than did those without term limits.[2]

The crosstab alone, however, does not clearly establish the reform as a causal factor. There is a slight increase in women among newcomers in term-limit states and a slight decrease in non-term-limit states, but the differences are small relative to the difference in the proportion of women across the two types of states among old-timers.

Moreover, to isolate any effect of term limits, it is necessary to control for other factors expected to affect the gender balance. Level of professionalization, as noted, is one such factor.[3] In addition, the demographic composition of specific state legislative districts can be expected to affect electoral prospects for women. It is known, for example, that women legislators are more liberal than are male legislators, which suggests that districts with large minority populations and districts with relatively highly educated respondents might more often elect women. More to the point, the South has historically had fewer women in its state legislatures, and this region is slightly underrepresented in the proportion of term-limit states.[4] In addition, various other factors, such as the partisan makeup of the district and structural factors such as the chamber (upper or lower), might affect the election of women. As noted in the opening chapter, the presence of so many factors that might help account for variations in the dependent variable (here whether the district is represented by a male or a female) calls for a multivariate test.

The results of that test are shown in table 2.2. For a technical reason—the fact that the dependent variable is dichotomous—we use logit

TABLE 2.1. Percentage of Women in State Legislatures, by Cohort and Term-Limit Status of the State

| Cohort | States | | Total |
	Non-term limit	Term limit	
Old Timers	18.2 (1,487)	23.2 (707)	19.8 (2,194)
Newcomers	16.5 (443)	24.6 (276)	19.6 (719)
Total	17.8 (1,930)	23.6 (983)	19.7 (2,913)

Source: 1995 Survey of State Legislators.

Note: *N*'s shown in parentheses.

analysis in this table but ordinary least squares (OLS) in some other tables. In either event, the most relevant figures are the coefficients for the variables of interest, in this case the coefficients for the effects of cohort (NC versus OT) and term limits (TL versus NTL) on the likelihood of electing a female state legislator. Because we scored men as 1 and women as 2, a positive coefficient means that group (e.g., OTTLs) contained a greater

TABLE 2.2.   Gender of Old and New State Legislators in Term-Limit and Non-Term-Limit States

Dependent variable (logit analysis):			Sex		
Scale:			Men = 1; Women = 2		
Residual group:			OTNTL		
Legislative group			b		Standard error
OTTL			.44*		.14
NCNTL			-.27		.18
NCTL**			.46*		.19
Control Variables	b	s.e.		b	s.e.
Constant	-2.64*	.84	District characteristics		
Chamber	-0.03	.17	% Black	0.02*	.00
Professionalization	-0.38	.32	% Hispanic	0.02*	.01
Party control	-0.20	.12	% Asian	-0.00	.01
Size of district	-0.00*	.00	% Democratic	0.00	.00
Size of Chamber	0.00	.00	% college educated	0.03*	.01
South	-0.85*	.18	% age 55 and over	0.02	.01
District party ID	-0.01	.00	% farm sector	-0.03*	.01
Legislator's party	-0.38*	.14	% service sector	0.01	.01
			% government sector	0.00	.02
			Avg. household inc.	0.00	.00
N = 2,097 Model χ^2 = 189*					

Source: 1995 Survey of State Legislators.

*$p < .05$

** Difference between NCTLs and NCNTLs: $p < .05$

proportion of women (subject to our standard controls) than the residual group (OTNTLs).

The results are most easily interpreted if we use the coefficients to order the groups from least likely to most likely to elect women, that is: NCNTL .27, OTNTL (0), OTTL .44, and NCTL .46. With professionalization, district demographics, and other variables controlled, women are better represented in term-limit states among both old-timers and newcomers. Moreover, the gender gap between term-limit and non-term-limit states is somewhat larger among newcomers than among old-timers. Strikingly, however, this phenomenon does not occur because newcomers in term-limit states are more likely to be female than are old-timers but because newcomers in non-term-limit states are less likely to be female than are old-timers.

That the non-term-limit states were less likely to have women in the state legislatures in 1995 (despite overall historic trends toward more women) may reflect the fact that Republicans made sharp gains in the 1994 elections in many states, whereas women are better represented among Democratic legislators. If so, it is possible that term-limit states retained their previous share of women because women candidates in term-limit states were somehow immune from what would otherwise would have been a retrogressive trend.[5] Term limits prompted many senior legislators to retire preemptively in the early 1990s, even before they were legally prohibited from reelection. Because such senior legislators are overwhelmingly male, their departures may have mitigated the effects of an electoral atmosphere that otherwise was not favorable to female candidates.

In short, the states that adopted term limits in the early 1990s have elected more women to state legislative office than the states that did not adopt limits, even before term limits came along. In the first years after limits were adopted, the electoral environment was not favorable to women, yet their setbacks were less in TL than in NTL states, so term limits may have helped women candidates shore up the gains they made in the 1980s and early 1990s. The statistical evidence is suggestive but not conclusive.

Ideology

Apart from demographic changes, we also sought evidence for the effects of term limits on legislator ideology. Both advocates and opponents of reform have suggested that term limits might create a political environment hostile toward big government. However, term limits were adopted across the country during a period of widespread anti-incumbent sentiment in the early 1990s. It is therefore reasonable to question whether term limits were merely a symptom of this general skepticism toward government or, alternatively, whether they contributed to such attitudes among legislators by encouraging the election of candidates who are less likely to aspire to government careers.

Both our interviews and our survey data suggest that term limits are more a symptom than a cause of any changes in legislators' attitudes. As Senate majority leader Chelley Pingree (D-ME) put it,

> I don't think that there was a different kind of candidate running because of term limits, but there have [been] different kinds of candidates running in the last couple of elections—and maybe it was a result of the ideology that created term limits—but people with less respect for the process, people who wanted rapid change and came in on a wave of change. I don't know that term limits attracted those people. . . . I think term limits were partly born out of this idea that people in politics are pond scum, that this is the resting place for bad guys.

There is good reason to believe that the attitude described by Pingree was widespread among both candidates and voters during this period and was not unique to term-limit states: polls in the early 1990s showed strong public support for term limits across states with and without term-limits initiatives on the ballot (Dick and Lott 1996).[6] If there was a general antigovernment shift in public opinion in the early and mid-1990s, we are likely to see it reflected in the ideology of state legislators first elected during this period. But we can only attribute an independent effect to term limits if the ideological shift is larger in term-limit states than in non-term-limit states, controlling for alternative explanatory factors. Once again, the results here are generally negative.

Our most straightforward test was simply to ask our survey respondents to place themselves on a seven-point scale ranging from extremely liberal to extremely conservative. On this measure, newcomers are slightly more conservative than old-timers (with controls in place), but there is no significant difference between either old-timers or newcomers in term-limit and non-term-limit states. Nor are there any differences among the groups in the degree of ideological extremism (measured as the legislator's self-placement score "folded" at 4, the midpoint). By these measures, the term-limit reform appears to have had no effect on legislators' ideology.

We also asked for legislators' positions on four specific policy issues. The results here show only marginally more variation across our groups of legislators than does the general ideology question, and there is no evidence of a systematic effect of term limits. Specifically, we asked legislators to rank their level of agreement, using a five-point scale ranging from strong agreement (1) to strong disagreement (5), with the following statements:

"It is important to protect a woman's right to abortion."
"We should cut taxes, even if it means deep cuts in
    government programs."
"We should abolish the death penalty."
"We should have mandatory prayer in the public schools."

The regression results for each of these four issues are shown in tables 2.3a–d. Because, on the survey instrument, the scale was laid out from left to right, with "disagree" taking the higher score, the regression coefficients are somewhat counterintuitive and a little tricky to interpret.

There is no trace of a term-limits effect on the questions regarding abortion and tax cuts. On the former, legislators from non-term-limit states appear to be slightly more pro-life than those from term-limit states, and newcomers in both types of states are barely perceptibly more pro-life than are old-timers; but the patterns across states mirror each other perfectly, and in any case, none of these differences reaches conventional levels of statistical significance. A similar picture emerges with respect to tax cuts. Newcomers in both types of states favor tax cuts—even if they require cuts in government services—more than do old-timers. Legislators in term-limit states favor cuts more than do their counterparts in non-term-limit states; but the magnitude of the difference between old-timers and newcomers is nearly identical across both types of states, suggesting that the differences among groups are driven entirely by the trend toward fiscal conservatism in the early 1990s, without any evidence of a separate term-limits effect.

On the death penalty and school prayer, there is somewhat more evidence of a term-limits effect, although it is not the one suggested by most accounts of the term-limits movement. Term-limit state legislators favor the death penalty more than do their counterparts in non-term-limit states. There is virtually no difference between the cohorts of legislators from term-limit states, however, whereas in non-term-limit states newcomers favor the death penalty substantially more than do old-timers. Newcomers are also generally more supportive of school prayer than are old-timers, and legislators in non-term-limit states are more supportive than those in term-limit states; yet the difference between cohorts is slightly more pronounced in non-term-limit states than in term-limit states.

On the death penalty and school prayer, the swing toward social conservatism among state legislators first elected in the early 1990s was

TABLE 2.3a. Differences between Old-Timers and Newcomers and between Legislators in Term-Limit and Non-Term-Limit States in Response to "It is important to protect a woman's right to abortion."

Dependent variable:	Protect right to abortion
Scale:	Agree strongly = 1, to Disagree strongly = 5
Residual group:	OTNTL

Legislative group	b	Standard error
OTTL	-.15	.08
NCNTL	.03	.10
NCTL	-.13	.13

Control Variables	b	s.e.		b	s.e.
Constant	1.30*	.48	District characteristics		
Chamber	-0.12	.09	% Black	-0.02*	.00
Professionalization	0.63*	.17	% Hispanic	-0.02*	.00
Party control	0.04	.07	% Asian	-0.01*	.00
Size of district	-0.00	.00	% Democratic	-0.00	.00
Size of chamber	-0.00*	.00	% college educated	-0.05*	.01
South	0.64*	.09	% age 55 and over ov	-0.02*	.01
District safeness	0.01*	.00	% farm sector	-0.02*	.01
Legislator's party	1.16*	.08	% service sector	0.01*	.01
Tenure	0.01	.02	% government sector	-0.00	.00
			Avg. household inc.	0.00	.00

$N = 2,200$ Adj. $R^2 = .25$

Source: 1995 Survey of State Legislators.

* $p < .05$

** Difference between NCTLs and NCNTLs: $p < .01$

TABLE 2.3b. Differences between Old-Timers and Newcomers and between Legislators in Term-Limit and Non-Term-Limit States in Response to "We should cut taxes, even if it means deep cuts in government programs."

Dependent variable:	Cut taxes
Scale:	Agree strongly = 1, to Disagree strongly = 5
Residual group:	OTNTL

Legislative group	b	Standard error
OTTL	.14*	.06
NCNTL	-.19*	.08
NCTL	-.03	.10

Control Variables	b	s.e.		b	s.e.
Constant	4.56*	.37	District characteristics		
Chamber	0.20*	.07	% Black	0.01*	.00
Professionalization	-0.04	.13	% Hispanic	0.01*	.00
Party control	-0.07	.06	% Asian	-0.00	.00
Size of district	0.00	.00	% Democratic	0.01*	.00
Size of chamber	0.00	.00	% college educated	0.02*	.00
South	-0.32*	.07	% age 55 and over	0.01	.00
District safeness	0.00	0.00	% farm sector	-0.00	.00
Legislator's party	-1.61*	.06	% service sector	-0.01	.00
Tenure	0.04*	.02	% government sector	0.01	.01
			Avg. household inc.	0.00*	.00
$N = 2,212$ Adj. $R^2 = .41$					

Source: 1995 Survey of State Legislators.

* $p < .05$

** Difference between NCTLs and NCNTLs: $p < .01$

TABLE 2.3c. Differences between Old-Timers and Newcomers and between Legislators in Term-Limit and Non-Term-Limit States in Response to "We should abolish the death penalty."

Dependent variable:			Abolish death penalty		
Scale:			Agree strongly = 1, to Disagree strongly = 5		
Residual group:			OTNTL		

Legislative group			b		Standard error
OTTL			.27*		.07
NCNTL			.23*		.09
NCTL			.30*		.11

Control Variables	b	s.e.		b	s.e.
Constant	3.19*	.42	District characteristics		
Chamber	-0.18*	.08	% Black	-0.01	.00
Professionalization	-0.13	.15	% Hispanic	-0.01*	.00
Party control	0.28*	.06	% Asian	-0.01	.00
Size of district	0.00	.00	% Democratic	-0.01*	.00
Size of chamber	0.00	.00	% college educated	-0.04*	.00
South	0.87*	.08	% age 55 and over	-0.01*	.01
District safeness	-0.00*	.00	% farm sector	0.00	.00
Legislator's party	1.10*	.07	% service sector	0.00	.00
Tenure	0.01	.02	% government sector	0.01	.01
			Avg. household inc.	0.00*	.00
$N = 2,208$ Adj. $R^2 = .29$					

Source: 1995 Survey of State Legislators.

* $p < .05$

** Difference between NCTLs and NCNTLs: $p < .01$

TABLE 2.3d. Differences between Old-Timers and Newcomers and between Legislators in Term-Limit and Non-Term-Limit States in Response to "We should have mandatory prayer in the public schools."

Dependent variable:			Mandatory school prayer		
Scale:			Agree strongly = 1, to Disagree strongly = 5		
Residual group:			OTNTL		

Legislative group			b		Standard error
OTTL			.23*		.07
NCNTL			-.19*		.09
NCTL			.15		.11

Control Variables	b	s.e.		b	s.e
Constant	4.85*	.40	District characteristics		
Chamber	0.07	.08	% Black	0.00	.00
Professionalization	-0.15	.14	% Hispanic	0.01*	.00
Party control	-0.04	.06	% Asian	0.00	.00
Size of district	-0.00	.00	% Democratic	-0.00	.00
Size of chamber	0.00	.00	% college educated	0.03*	.00
South	-0.53*	.08	% age 55 and over	0.02*	.01
District safeness	-0.01*	.00	% farm sector	-0.00	.01
Legislator's party	-0.85*	.07	% service sector	0.01	.00
Tenure	-0.05*	.02	% government sector	0.00	.01
			Avg. household inc.	0.00	.00
$N = 2{,}202$ Adj. $R^2 = .17$					

Source: 1995 Survey of State Legislators.

* $p < .05$

** Difference between NCTLs and NCNTLs: $p < .01$

slightly less pronounced in term-limit states than in non-term-limit states. This finding runs contrary to the usual arguments that associate term limits with conservatism. We urge caution, however, in interpreting these results. First, the differences between these shifts represent between one-tenth and two-tenths of one point on the five-point scale used in the survey instrument. Second, we find evidence of a term-limits effect on only two of the four specific policy questions and none whatsoever on general ideological self-placement. In sum, the initial effects of term limits on state legislator ideology appear to be marginal, if not negligible. What evidence we do find of an effect, however, suggests that term limits dampened rather than amplified the trend toward social conservatism that characterized elections in the early 1990s.

Effects on Elections

Turnover and Partisanship

Apart from effects on the demographic and ideological characteristics of legislators, term limits will inevitably affect rates of turnover. Once limits kick in, term-limited states are almost certain to have a greater proportion of novice legislators and will have none with long and uninterrupted careers in any given chamber. With the data from 1995, however, we can see that increased turnover has begun even before term limits kicked in anywhere.

In reaching this conclusion, it is again important that we employ a multivariate model. Here we treated each state as a unit and regressed the proportion of first-term legislators on our standard set of state-level controls (adding a variable for the extent of district competitiveness in the state) as well as a dummy variable to distinguish term-limit states from non-term-limit states. The result shows that already in 1995, legislatures in term-limit states had 9 percent more freshmen than those in non-term-limit states with analogous demographic and institutional characteristics. In the next chapter, we show that old-timers in term-limit states are more likely to express intentions not to run for reelection than are old-timers in non-term-limit states, even before they reach their year of legal prohibition. Term limits thus appear to have had an anticipatory effect on turnover by discouraging senior legislators and opening up more legislative seats to newcomers.[7]

This particular anticipatory effect is likely to be short-lived because, according to our survey, newcomers in term-limit states are as likely as their counterparts in non-term-limit states to run for reelection at the end of their current terms. The anticipatory effect, however, will soon be replaced with the much larger, legal effect of term limits—mandating the removal of veteran legislators from office.

The inevitable effect on turnover will, in time, spill over onto the partisan composition of the state legislatures. Initially, there will be a partisan imbalance that will be pro-Republican. Because most term limits allow eight years of service and most were adopted by 1992, their initial victims will be legislators first elected in or before 1992, when Democrats dominated most state legislatures. Thus, through the year 2000, most legislators legally prohibited from reelection are Democrats. Beginning in 2002, however, when eight-year limits will remove legislators first elected in 1994, the bite of term limits should be felt by Republicans more than Democrats (assuming that the same proportion of Republicans and Democrats first elected in 1994 serve their full legal terms). Table 2.4 shows just how dramatic the partisan effects might be.

In the long run, the partisan impact of the reform should be to handicap the party that was most successful in the election that took place the term-limited number of years ago. From the perspective of the party system—as opposed to individual party advantage or disadvantage—the effect may be to constrain the duration of partisan tides. Should one party sweep a large majority of legislative seats in a given election or for a period of two or three elections, it will have relatively more legislators evicted by term limits just a few elections later. This situation does not guarantee a partisan reversal: the same party could still be favored on the basis of its issue positions. Yet these circumstances are likely to level the field by tak-

TABLE 2.4. Partisanship of Legislators by When Term Limits Kick In

Partisanship of legislators affected	Non-term-limit states	Legislators who will reach their term limit in:			
		1996–1998	2000	2002	2004 or later
Democrats (%)	51	54	52	45	37
Republicans (%)	50	46	48	55	63
N	1,859	177	383	391	83

Note: Calculations are based on when each legislator was first elected and when term limits go into effect in each state. Dates of first election were determined from our survey and from information provided by the National Council of State Legislatures.

ing away the advantages of incumbency, giving the minority party a greater opportunity to regain seats. Long periods of one-party domination of state legislatures may as a result be less frequent and may be replaced by shorter-term fluctuations as first one party then the other finds its incumbents forced from office.

Competitiveness

Claims about the expected effects of term limits on the competitiveness of state legislative elections, like those about composition in general, have been diverse and dramatic. Proponents have projected more competitive elections both because of increased numbers of open-seat contests and because of the decreased electoral advantage accrued by long-term incumbency. They have also claimed that term limits will diminish campaign spending by reducing the value of incumbency both to officeholders and to contributors. Skeptics have countered that term limits might actually decrease competitiveness in those races where incumbents are allowed to run, as potential challengers await the guarantee of an open seat within the next electoral cycle or two. Opponents have also argued that as term-limited politicians run for new posts with new constituencies in which their name recognition is low, the demand for campaign funds will actually increase.

The most dramatic empirical evidence for the former position is presented by Daniel and Lott (1997), whose study of California elections concludes that term limits have both increased competitiveness and decreased campaign spending. Daniel and Lott's results are based on California state legislative election results from 1978 through 1996. Their focus on patterns of competitiveness in one state over time, however, leads them to dubious conclusions. Their goal is to evaluate the effect of term limits on a number of dependent variables: the probability of incumbent defeat, vote differential between the top two candidates, the number of candidates contesting races, and campaign spending. Daniel and Lott include statistical controls for standard factors expected to affect competitiveness, such as whether the incumbent ran unopposed in the past, the past margin of victory, incumbent tenure, and presidential election years.

The central problem is that Daniel and Lott's method of isolating the effect of term limits is limited to creating a dummy variable for the elections in 1992 and 1994, along with another for the 1990 election in which term limits were originally adopted. Finding that the probability of incumbent defeats rose, victory margins decreased, contested races increased, and spending declined in the early 1990s, they attribute the results entirely to term limits. Yet basing such a conclusion exclusively on data from one state ignores completely the nationwide trend toward anti-incumbency in both term-limit and non-term-limit states in the early 1990s.

While investigating incumbency effects more broadly, we created a statistical model to estimate how much incumbency increases the probability of election for state legislative candidates, controlling for district demographics, legislative professionalization, and differences in electoral rules. Drawing on data from 1992–94 from forty-eight states, we concluded that certain electoral rules—notably the existence of single-member versus multimember districts and two- versus four-year terms—made a considerable difference in reelection probabilities. Yet we found no effect of term limits on the probability that incumbents win reelection (Carey, Niemi, and Powell 2000). It would appear, then, that Daniel and Lott's results are a product of their limited data and questionable specification of term-limit effects.

Our interviewees, though quick to point to increased levels of turnover and open seats where term limits had already kicked in (Gwadosky in Maine, Bill Lockyer in California), supported the idea that term limits discourage challenges to incumbents eligible for reelection. This was particularly the case among Maine legislators, who at the time of the interviews had already faced two electoral cycles after limits were adopted and the first in which limits were enforced. Incumbents of both parties perceived decreased willingness of viable challengers to step forward during the most recent elections and attributing this phenomenon to the imminent certainty that the seats would be open soon (Pingree). According to Lawrence,

> Maine has four-term limits, and you really only have one shot to challenge an incumbent, because it's usually after their first term. You know, if you can't defeat them after their first term, people tend to say, "Well, they're in there for the eight years." So it's kind of converted a two-year term into an eight-year term.

Maine's House minority leader, James Donnelly (R), concurred:

> With strong incumbents, heading into their third and fourth terms, most people are willing to wait them out. . . . I think the first two terms a representative has will be competitive; and the third and fourth, if they do the things they're supposed to do right, will have very light competition. Then when the seat becomes open, due to term limits, there will be heavy competition again.

Similarly with respect to campaign spending, incumbent legislators expressed the skeptics' view that the demand for money increases as a result of term limits. The rationale was the same in the least- and the most-professionalized legislatures where we interviewed (Lawrence; Lockyer). It was best summed up by an assembly member from California, where state legislative campaigns are the most professionalized and expensive in the nation:

> *Legislator:* I don't think term limits [decrease the importance of money to legislators] at all. And, if you feel like you're moving on, it's just the opposite. And I think I'm a good example of that. Given the district that I represent—a low-turnout, minority district—I don't have to raise very much money to get reelected. I might get away with raising $50,000–100,000, just to be safe, but I don't need more than that, and even that may be overkill. Then, of course, the leadership wants me to raise a little bit more to give to the caucus and to give to other members, and you start doing that. But now, I think "I may have to move on from here. I may have to run statewide or for a regional office, or whatever." Now, I don't need to raise $100,000—I need to raise several million. If I think, "Well, I want to run for Congress, but that's half a million dollar price tag," I have to start meeting a lot of people *today,* even if I may not need them until later, I need to start developing my Rolodex now.
>
> *Interviewer:* Is that starting to have an effect on people's activities in the assembly?
>
> *Legislator:* Well, I think there is a relationship between—I think people are very aware of who champions what issues and what kind of resources they have.

It should not be surprising, of course, that incumbent legislators—the group most adversely affected by term limits—display skepticism toward the reform. We certainly do not claim that interview responses are free from bias in this regard. Nevertheless, bearing in mind the nature of the source, these opinions warrant consideration. They complement statistical analyses by articulating explicitly the mechanism by which term limits might decrease competitiveness in some races while simultaneously increasing the demand for money. In so doing, these responses also suggest how statistical models could be refined to focus with greater precision on specific types of races where term limits might affect competition.

Conclusion

The most striking result of this chapter is the dearth of evidence for direct effects of term limits on the demographic and ideological composition of state legislatures. In surveys conducted three electoral cycles after the term limits movement began (and interviews conducted an additional cycle later), we find no differences attributable to term limits in the race, religion, age, occupation, education, or income level of recently elected legislators. There appears to be a slightly positive effect (or rather, a mitigation in the negative trend of the 1994 electoral cycle) among term-limit states in the tendency to elect women to state legislative office. There is also limited suggestion from our surveys that term limits mitigated the trend toward social conservatism among legislators first elected in the 1992 and 1994 election cycles. In both cases, however, the statistical results here are spotty enough to warrant caution.

Term limits will necessarily affect turnover rates in state legislatures and with that, the amount of experience among their members. Indeed, we found that limits contributed to increased levels of turnover in the states that adopted such limits even before they took effect. Increased turnover is also likely to mean that there will be effects on partisanship: a party that wins a large majority of legislators statewide or nationwide may lose a disproportionate number of seats some years later because the legislators will no longer have the advantage of incumbency. By changing party composition, this secondary effect could also indirectly influence the ideological balance in legislatures, but it cannot do so consistently in one direction, as presumed by some term-limit advocates.

Table 2.5 summarizes the effects of term limits on legislative composition and legislative elections for which we looked, whether we found any trace of such effects, and the evidence on which we base our conclusions. Overall, term limits appear to have little effect on the composition of state legislatures, except in the obvious sense that turnover and the number of first- and second-term legislators will increase as limits go into effect in more and more states. Term limits might help a few more women win office. Limits may encourage a cyclical pattern of competition for open seats, and they may drive campaign costs up, although these projections are speculative. The most likely scenario is that over the next decade, there will be increasing numbers of new faces in the state capitols of term-limited states, but the new faces will look remarkably like those they have replaced.

TABLE 2.5. Summary Effects of Term Limits on Legislative Composition and Elections

Projected Effect on	Detected Effect of Term Limits	Evidence
Income level	none	1995 survey data
Level of education	none	1995 survey data
Age	none	1995 survey data
Race	none	1995 survey data
Religious affiliation	none	1995 survey data
Occupational background	none	1995 survey data
Overall ideology	none	1995 survey data
Ideological extremism	none	1995 survey data
Social conservatism	mitigated swing toward social conservatism in mid-1990s (slightly)	1995 survey data
Sex	help women candidates (slightly)	1995 survey data
Partisan turnover	throw out more Democrats than Republicans through 2000, more Republicans than Democrats thereafter	1995 survey data
Electoral competitiveness	discourage challenges against eligible incumbents; encourage challengers to await open seats	legislator interviews
Campaign costs	increase costs by generating more open-seat contests, encouraging politicians to broaden electoral base	legislator interviews

CHAPTER 3

Behavioral Effects

The recruitment and election of a new breed of state legislator was largely unsubstantiated by the survey and interview data presented in chapter 2. Term limits had swept through 40 percent of the states by the time of our fieldwork, and various changes were widely reported in anticipation of their first enforcement in 1996 and 1998. Yet as far as we could tell, the demographic and ideological makeup of state legislatures was not immediately altered by the reform, and there was no suggestion—except possibly for small effects on the percentage of women elected—that such changes would occur in the future.

The expectation of a new type of legislator, however, hardly exhausts the predicted effects of the term-limit reform. Even in the absence of compositional changes, it is thought that legislative behavior will change as a result of changing incentive structures facing politicians. The timetable for such changes was thought to be slower than that for compositional matters, yet even here some anticipatory effects were projected. Therefore, in this chapter, we investigate the set of expectations surrounding legislative behavior. It is noteworthy that although our results here are mixed, we find stronger evidence of a term-limits effect with respect to behavior than with respect to composition.

Expectations about behavioral effects of term limits are quite extensive. Term-limit advocates have argued first that the reform will encourage legislators to spend less time focusing on their own reelection prospects and more time on legislative activities (Glazer and Wattenberg 1996). Thus, we would expect to see legislators spend less time on campaigning, fund-raising, performing constituent service, and other types of electioneering and more time studying and developing legislation and building legislative coalitions.

Others have argued that term limits will affect the extent to which legislators focus on specific issues rather than on being active across many policy areas, although predictions here vary. Some scholars contend that legislators who know that their careers will be short will specialize to enact their personal policy agenda before their time is up (Herrick, Moore, and Hibbing 1994). Others hold that term limits will reduce the incentive to develop the kind of policy expertise in a particular area that can translate into authority within specialized legislative committees (Rosenthal 1992; Capell 1996). Our survey results account in detail for how legislators budget their time among a range of activities, allowing us to evaluate hypotheses about both legislators' reelection or legislative focus and their degree of specialization.

Reform advocates also argue that by severing the electoral connection between politicians and constituents, term limits will alter legislators' priorities, encouraging them to consider broader interests than those of their districts, thus generating Burkean legislators who are motivated more by conscience than by the demands of clamoring interest groups (Will 1992). We evaluate these claims based on survey questions that ask legislators to evaluate the relative priority they accord to the interests of their districts, their states, and the demands of their consciences in making policy decisions.

The argument that term-limited legislators will be less responsive to electoral constituencies is based on the premise that legislators do not aspire to careers in elected office—the celebrated citizen-legislator championed by term-limits proponents (Mitchell 1991; Petracca 1991; Novak 1993). Yet even under term limits, legislators may remain committed to political careers by running for other elective offices, accepting appointive positions, or working as lobbyists or consultants on political issues. In furthering these goals legislators may be responsive to other constituencies or interests even if not to their own district. In contrast to these career politicians, we would expect less career oriented politicians to be more likely to continue to hold jobs outside the legislature while in office. Consequently, we asked legislators whether they thought of politics as a career, whether they intended to run for reelection, their eventual aspirations to serve in other political offices and positions, and whether they held jobs outside the legislature.

If changes in legislative behavior are a result of new incentive structures, newcomers to the legislature are more likely than are old-timers to demonstrate this effect because they have not yet established a legislative style. However, old-timers in term-limit states may also be significantly affected because, after all, they will eventually be out of jobs just as surely as the newcomers. Therefore, to test hypotheses about legislative behavior, we need to rely on the same methodology as in chapter 2—that is, we need to distinguish the four groups of legislators defined by their election in TL or NTL states and by their status as OTs or NCs. It is also appropriate, as earlier, to control for each state's political, demographic, and economic conditions.

There is one added feature, however. In chapter 2 we were interested in differences between OTNTLs and OTTLs primarily as a check to verify that any differences between NCNTLs and NCTLs—the prime comparison groups when looking for compositional effects—were in fact the product of term limits. Contrasts between OTNTLs and OTTLs will serve that purpose here as well. But with respect to behavior, as we noted, we anticipate reform-caused differences between old-timers in TL and NTL states because all those who serve in term-limited legislatures have had their career prospects curtailed and may alter their behavior in response. By controlling, as we do, for a comprehensive set of variables, we have reasonable assurance that observed differences between OTTLs and OTNTLs are the product of term limits rather than the product of some omitted variable.[1] Recognizing, then, that our comparisons are slightly more complex than in the previous chapter, let us turn to the first of the expected effects.

In an effort to determine whether term limits affect the activities to which legislators devote time and effort, we asked survey respondents to evaluate how much time they spend on each of the following activities, using a five-point scale from 1 (a great deal) to 5 (hardly any):

- developing new legislation
- studying proposed legislation
- building coalitions within own party to pass legislation
- building coalitions across parties to pass legislation
- campaigning/fund-raising
- keeping in touch with constituents
- helping constituents with problems with government
- making sure district gets fair share of government money and projects

In the popular debate over term limits, each of these areas has received some attention. Proponents have argued that term-limited legislators will spend more time on policy-making activities, such as the first four listed here, and less time on reelection-oriented activities, such as the final four. Others have suggested that term-limited legislators will be quicker to develop their legislative agendas to realize their policy goals during their short period in office (Glazer and Wattenberg 1996). Proponents of limits generally regard this development as an advantage of the reform and associate it with policy innovation. Opponents contend that it will mean that legislatures will be flooded with proposals from novice politicians who have yet to develop sufficient understanding of complex public-policy issues. Opponents also suggest that term limits will increase the tendency of ambitious politicians who aspire to higher office to seek the political limelight as individuals, rather than as team players, and so will undermine incentives for cooperation and coalition-building both within and across parties.

Policy-Making Activities

Among our interviewees, the sense that term limits undermine incentives for cooperation and increase legislative individualism was pervasive. This reasoning followed two tracks, changing relationships among legislators and the relationship between legislators and the public. The first line of reasoning was summed up by an anonymous California legislator:

> There's a tremendous loss of the glue that makes the legislature work in terms of personal relationships—not only across partisan lines, but even within the caucus, and you just don't hear members saying, "I've served with this guy." I used to hear guys say all the time, "I've served with X for a long time, and I'd give my life for X." But they don't do it anymore; you just don't hear it. Now it's more like, "I don't know who these guys are." It's just looking out for Number One. And "I have to think about what I'm running for next, and I have to think about how this is going to play in that district." Basically, all the personal relations that made up the glue, respecting each other, being willing to accommodate fellow members, even within a caucus, [are] just gone.

There is an element here of game-theoretical arguments about the difficulty of sustaining cooperation in games with fixed endpoints and in games in which there is mutual uncertainty among players about the preferences of others (Barro 1973; Calvert 1993). The idea is that both knowledge of the political dispositions of others and the expectation that concessions granted today can be repaid on future projects are essential to cooperation among legislators.

The second theme from the interviews was that cooperation and coalition-building are undermined by the need for ambitious term-limited legislators to extend their political reputations to new constituencies. The result, echoed in interview after interview, is an increased emphasis on staking out highly visible positions on issues salient to voters, without regard for progress on a viable legislative agenda. Senator Stanley Rosenberg (D-MA) explicitly summed up the shifting incentives and corresponding political strategies:

Many people are looking more seriously at running for statewide office and running for Congress. People are clearly doing that, and that's affecting the lawmaking process, because when you think in those terms, you're not only thinking about "What do I need to do to honestly represent those who have elected me?" but "If I'm going broaden that pool, that base, what am I going to have to add or to subtract from my agenda, or my performance or my style?" or "What accomplishments will I need?" And so I've started to see people doing more of that. . . . If you're running for statewide office and crime is the big issue in the office you want to run for, you believe you need a profile as being a crime fighter. But it's not the top priority or even a high priority in your district. Suddenly, you start trying to get a committee assignment or add some projects or pick up some legislation or become a high-profile spokesperson on something in crime, so you can begin to develop a regional or statewide image, or add that to your image. That would be just one example. [The question becomes,] "Just what do I have to do to broaden myself?"

By Rosenberg's account, changes in a legislator's priorities as a result of term limits could alter levels of attention devoted to various policy issues but do not necessarily imply a decreased willingness to cooperate. House Speaker Thomas Finneran (D-MA) was more discouraged:

I'm troubled by, generally speaking, the method or manner in which people try to vault from the legislature to this new higher office. Often it's done at the expense of their fellow legislators with what I call positioning legislation or positioning amendments. Things that the candidate himself—let's say it's Tom Finneran, legislator, now running for state treasurer or auditor or something like that—things that I know in my heart of hearts, if I was to go into a confessional with you I'd say, "This bill's the biggest piece of shit in the world and we should never do it." But it elevates me, it gives me a profile, gives me a stature that I don't have if I continue to vote the responsible way against this because we can't afford it or because of this or that consequence.

In addition to demonstrating that taking positions (see Mayhew 1974) erodes cooperation in the chamber, Finneran's comment also suggests that the legislative individualism encouraged by term limits generates poorly thought out policy proposals. Other interviewees expressed similar opinions. In part, the consensus that policy proposals are uninformed may be driven by disdain among the committee chairs and party leaders we interviewed for the relative lack of experience among their post–term limit colleagues, but this consensus also appears to be driven by a conviction that term limits create a general disincentive toward studying legislative proposals and acquiring policy expertise. According to Senate President Bill Lockyer (D-CA),

> There is a little more emphasis on simple conceptual bills that are politically popular that don't represent some complicated program-matic change or something that doesn't qualify for press attention. And part of that is just the need to continue to get better known, to try to run for higher office. So I see more of that happening than before. It happened before, too, but there is more of it now.

The anonymous California legislator was both more blunt and more specific:

> I'm serious when I say that it's amateur hour. People don't know the rules. They don't know substance. So they tend to focus on—well, everything's sort of rhetorical, and if you don't know anything about tax policy and you can't talk about it intellectually, then everything is either, well, "The chamber's for it or against it," or "Tax reform peo-ple are for it or against it." Or just that "It's good or not good for my district." There's not much intellectual give and take. . . . I think that in California, it has been true that people did not want to wrestle with the truly difficult subjects like, well, the tax law is a good one because, well, it's so boring that you get no credit for it. Nobody wants to become an expert in local finance or property taxes. I mean, people are just loathe to take a stand on things that can be demagogued by the other side—like with Prop. 13. You don't even want to talk about things that might be wrong with Prop. 13. So, one, you don't want to start work on projects that might take several years to develop because you don't have the time to do it. You just focus on short-term things. Two, people don't want to think about how to reform the property-tax system because they're not familiar with how it works, so you just end up tinkering at the margins.

All these opinions reflect the conviction that term limits alter attitudes toward legislative work. The legislators with whom we spoke, who were generally senior, overwhelmingly held that limits increase individualism and decrease incentives to become informed. Senate Appropriations chair Patrick Johnston (D-CA) even suggested that committee work ought to be redistributed according to a legislator's proximity to limits, so that those in their last term in the chamber should take on more-complex but lower-profile policy issues, leaving high-profile but less-complex issues to junior legislators eligible for reelection to their current office. Johnston's suggestion appears to contradict the beliefs of those quoted earlier that the incentive toward electioneering is stronger among those immediately confronting term limits than among those eligible for reelection. It is also worth noting that, despite his suggestion for reallocating workloads, Johnston did not see any evidence of such selfless behavior by senior legislators in California.

Minor differences aside, there was greater consensus among our interview subjects that term limits generate disincentives toward cooperative legislative work than on almost any other subject. This particular consensus is not supported, however, by the survey responses to our questions on how legislators spend their time. On the two questions about coalition-building (within one's own party and across parties) and on the question about studying proposed legislation, which inquires about attention to what others are doing, there was no statistically significant difference between the reported time spent by OTNTLs and OTTLs or by NCNTLs and NCTLs—that is, in neither the more experienced cohort nor the less experienced do our survey data register differences in what might be considered legislative collaboration and cooperation as a result of term limits. Of course, although these results fail to support the consensus among our interview subjects, it is equally noteworthy that they also fail to support the pro–term limits claim that legislators freed from the reelection imperative will devote more effort to crafting good policy.

The divergence between our survey and interview results likely results, at least in part, from bias in our interview group, which was comprised mostly of committee chairs and party leaders in term-limit states— generally senior legislators immediately confronting limits.[2] The interview sample was not intended to be unbiased, of course. Given limited time and resources, we looked for effects of term limits where we most expected to find them and explored those effects in detail. Thus, we should expect the interview results not to mirror those of the surveys but rather to amplify them and, in so doing, to throw light on the mechanics behind any positive results. In this case, however, the leaders are perhaps sensitive to differences that affect only a few individuals or to differences of which members themselves are unaware. Whether it is true that term-limited legislators are looking out for themselves in their work emphases and habits, legislative leaders see themselves as operating in a less-cooperative environment.

The fact that our survey respondents did not reveal differences in cooperative behavior should not lead one to believe that term limits were completely without consequences in the reports of ordinary legislators. We also asked legislators about the amount of time they spent developing new legislation, and there were differences suggesting that the reform affected newly elected legislators in term-limited states. To understand this difference, one needs to note first that OTNTLs and OTTLs do not differ in the attention they devote to developing new legislation, and both groups are more active than are NCs. Regardless of term limits, it appears that more-experienced legislators, who have shored up their electoral support, risen through their committee hierarchies, and developed policy expertise, devote more time to initiating legislation and command more of the resources that make policy leadership possible. In the interviews, this point was nicely articulated by Senator Rosenberg:

> We're not the legislators that were conceived of three hundred years ago. We're not lawmakers exclusively. We don't come here for a short period of time to make a bunch of laws and go home. We do economic development, we do public education, we do policy development, we do ribbon cutting, we do problem solving, we do interference with state agencies. Lawmaking is, for some legislators, occupying the vast minority of their time; for others, the majority. I find that the longer the people are around, the deeper they get into legislation and the better capacity they have because they are more solid back home. They can take bigger risks, they can strike out, they can do more homework, they attract more resources. We're staffed here, but minimally when you first come in. It grows in time.

It may be that the similarity in policy initiation between old-timers in term-limit and non-term-limit states results from the fact that this relative disparity in resources between cohorts is not affected by term limits or that term limits have not been in place long enough for the disparity to be erased. Alternatively, it could be that term limits affect different old-timers differently, with effects that cancel out, as Assemblyman Brian Thomas (R-WA) suggested:

> I've seen both types. . . . I've seen some people who are in their last term and they're so lazy, they're just doing nothing. And I've seen others who have, literally, introduced more legislation in this one term so far than in their whole careers before this, just because it's their last term. They go wild.

Whatever accounts for the similarities among old-timers, the more suggestive result from our surveys is that the difference between cohorts is less pronounced in term-limit states than in non-term-limit states. Although newcomers spend less time than old-timers on developing legislation, newcomers in term-limit states spend significantly more time developing new legislation than do newcomers in non-term-limit states (see table 3.1). This finding suggests that term limits do force legislators—especially those who have arrived with a fixed departure date and without the luxury of a period of apprenticeship—to push their policy priorities more quickly. Senator Rosenberg summed it up: "if you're coming here to do policy, you're going to have to get to it faster."

TABLE 3.1.   Time Spent Developing New Legislation by Old and New State Legislators in Term-Limit and Non-Term-Limit States

Dependent variable:			Developing new legislation		
Scale:			A great deal = 1, to Hardly any = 5		
Residual group:			OTNTL		
Legislative group			b		Standard error
OTTL			.01		.06
NCNTL			.37*		.07
NCTL**			.17*		.08
Control Variables	b	s.e.		b	s.e.
Constant	3.28*	.32	District characteristics		
Chamber	-0.11	.06	% Black	-0.00	.00
Professionalization	-0.04	.12	% Hispanic	-0.01*	.00
Party control	-0.06	.05	% Asian	-0.00	.00
Size of district	0.00	.00	% Democratic	0.00	.00
Size of chamber	0.00	.00	% college educated	0.00	.00
South	-0.11	.06	% age 55 and over	-0.01	.00
District safeness	0.00	.00	% farm sector	0.00	.00
Legislator's party	0.10	.05	% service sector	-0.01*	.00
			% government sector	0.00	.00
			Avg. household inc.	-0.00	.00
$N = 2,212$ Adj. $R^2 = .08$					

Source: 1995 Survey of State Legislators.

* $p < .05$

** Difference between NCTLs and NCNTLs: $p < .05$

Interview and survey results thus concur on this overarching point: term limits stimulate legislative initiatives. Interpretations of this phenomenon differ, however, according to whether one believes that legislative experience and a lack of time constraints are essential ingredients of sound policy judgment. Among our interview subjects, perhaps not surprisingly, there was little enthusiasm for increased levels of initiative among neophyte legislators, and the volume of new legislation was distinguished from its quality. According to Senator Dede Alpert (D-CA),

> I'm not sure about the bills that are ultimately passed, but certainly those introduced—it's like the same old ideas get recycled because nobody even knows they *are* the same old ideas. I still think, at this point, we're not seeing them necessarily be[ing] implemented. But you have to go through things and weed out more things now.

Reelection-Related Activities and Legislator-Constituent Relations

The second set of four questions regarding legislators' time budgets focused on activities conventionally associated with cultivating electoral support rather than policy development. On these questions, the survey data more consistently turn up differences attributable to term limits. With respect to campaigning and fund-raising, old-timers in term-limit states are substantially less active than are old-timers in non-term-limit states (see table 3.2). This reported disparity in campaign-related activity suggests that OTTLs are retiring from politics rather than gearing up campaigns for other office. Indeed, despite the fact that the vast majority of OTTLs surveyed would not be legally proscribed from office until 1998, 2000, or beyond, even as of 1995 they reported being far less likely than non-term-limited legislators to intend to run for reelection to their present offices when their current terms expired (see table 3.3). Evidently, the mere presence of term limits has made service in state legislatures sufficiently unattractive to many OTs as to suggest preemptive retirement.

This deterrent effect was not evident among the newer cohorts of legislators. NCTLs were as likely as NCNTLs to intend to run for reelection (table 3.3) and are equally active in campaigning and fund-raising (table 3.2). Newcomers in term-limit states know that they cannot stay in office for very many years, but they are eager to stay for at least a few terms. As the current NCTLs approach their own prohibitions on reelection, it will be interesting to see whether they remain as active as their corresponding cohort in non-term-limit states or whether these legislators cut back on reelection-related activities, as have OTTLs.

"Keeping in touch with constituents" and doing casework (i.e., helping constituents with problems with government) are other activities about which our survey inquired that are generally regarded as electorally oriented (Cain, Ferejohn, and Fiorina 1987). While the results for the four sets of legislators vary somewhat from one indicator to another, they are consistent with each other and with the results for campaigning and fundraising in suggesting small but likely effects of term limits. First, OTTLs report spending less time than others communicating with constituents (see table 3.4). This finding is consistent with their reduced campaigning

TABLE 3.2. Time Spent Campaigning and Fund-Raising by Old and New State Legislators in Term-Limit and Non-Term-Limit States

Dependent variable:			Campaigning/fund-raising		
Scale:			A great deal = 1, to Hardly any = 5		
Residual group:			OTNTL		
Legislative group			b		Standard error
OTTL			.22*		.06
NCNTL			.13		.08
NCTL			.15		.09
Control Variables	b	s.e.		b	s.e.
Constant	3.43*	.36	District characteristics		
Chamber	0.14*	.07	% Black	0.00	.00
Professionalization	-0.62*	.13	% Hispanic	0.00	.00
Party control	0.05	.05	% Asian	0.00	.00
Size of district	0.00	.00	% Democratic	0.00	.00
Size of chamber	0.00	.00	% college educated	0.00	.00
South	-0.05	.07	% age 55 and over	0.00	.01
District safeness	0.00	.00	% farm sector	0.01	.01
Legislator's party	0.07	.06	% service sector	-0.01*	.00
Tenure	0.05*	.02	% government sector	-0.01	.01
			Avg. household inc.	0.00	.00
N = 2,202 Adj. R^2 = .07					

Source: 1995 Survey of State Legislators.

* $p < .05$

and fund-raising. Second, NCTLs appear be less engaged than NCNTLs both in keeping in touch with constituents and in casework (see table 3.5)—that is, even though they are as interested as anyone else in running for reelection while they can and are devoting as much time as newcomers in NTL states to campaigning and fund-raising, newly elected legislators in TL states are marginally less likely to pay attention to their constituents.[3]

TABLE 3.3. Intentions to Run for Reelection, When Present Term Expires, of Old and New State Legislators in Term-Limit and Non-Term-Limit States

Dependent variable:			Intention to run for reelection		
Scale:			Definitely = 1, Probably = 2, Probably not = 3, Definitely not = 4		
Residual group:			OTNTL		
Legislative group			b		Standard error
OTTL			.21*		.04
NCNTL			.10*		.05
NCTL			.08		.06
Control Variables	b	s.e.		b	s.e.
Constant	1.50*	.25	District Characteristics		
Chamber	0.16*	.05	% Black	-0.00*	.00
Professionalization	-0.62*	.09	% Hispanic	0.01	.00
Party control	-0.02	.04	% Asian	-0.00	.00
Size of district	0.00*	.00	% Democratic	-0.00	.00
Size of chamber	0.00*	.00	% college educated	0.01*	.00
South	-0.23*	.05	% age 55 and over	-0.00	.00
District safeness	-0.00	.00	% farm sector	0.01	.00
Legislator's party	-0.13*	.04	% service sector	0.00	.00
Tenure	0.07*	.01	% government sector	0.00	.01
Age	0.01*	.00	Avg. household inc.	0.00	.00
N = 2,133	Adj. R^2 = .15				

Source: 1995 Survey of State Legislators.

* $p < .05$

The most striking results from the survey questions on time budgets concern the effort legislators spend making sure their districts get their fair share of government money and projects (i.e., pork). OTTLs are substantially less active here than OTNTLs, again consistent with their lesser efforts at electioneering. Even more interesting, NCNTLs are substantially more active than OTNTLs in chasing pork, perhaps because these legislators' seats are less safe and because pork is harder to come by for

TABLE 3.4.   Time Spent Keeping in Touch with Constituents by Old and New State Legislators in Term-Limit and Non-Term-Limit States

Dependent variable:			Keeping in touch with constituents		
Scale:			A great deal = 1, to Hardly any = 5		
Residual group:			OTNTL		
Legislative group			b		Standard error
OTTL			.09*		.05
NCNTL			-.03		.06
NCTL			.09		.08
Control Variables	b	s.e.		b	s.e.
Constant	2.03*	.29	District characteristics		
Chamber	0.07	.06	% Black	0.00	.00
Professionalization	-1.14*	.10	% Hispanic	0.00	.00
Party control	0.04	.04	% Asian	0.00	.00
Size of district	0.00	.00	% Democratic	0.00	.00
Size of chamber	0.00	.00	% college educated	0.00	.00
South	-0.21*	.09	% age 55 and over	-0.01*	.00
District safeness	0.03*	.05	% farm sector	-0.01	.00
Legislator's party	-0.85*	.07	% service sector	0.00	.00
Tenure	0.00	.00	% government sector	0.00	.01
			Avg. Household inc.	0.00	.00
N = 2,208 Adj. R^2 = .11					

Source: 1995 Survey of State Legislators.

* $p < .056$

** Difference between NCTLs and NCNTLs: p = .06 (one-tailed).

junior than senior legislators. Most striking of all is that NCTLs report spending the least time of all on pork—almost half a point less than NCNTLs on a five-point scale (see table 3.6). This finding is particularly remarkable given that these two groups are equal in their intentions to run for reelection, suggesting that legislators in term-limit states are less intent on pork-barreling in their efforts to secure electoral support.[4]

TABLE 3.5.   Time Spent on Casework by Old and New State Legislators in Term-Limit and Non-Term-Limit States

Dependent variable:			Helping constituents with government problems		
Scale:			A great deal = 1, to Hardly any = 5		
Residual group:			OTNTL		
Legislative group			b		Standard error
OTTL			.01		.05
NCNTL			.09		.06
NCTL**			.22*		.08
Control Variables	b	s.e.		b	s.e.
Constant	1.71*	.29	District characteristics		
Chamber	-0.02	.06	% Black	0.00	.00
Professionalization	-1.05*	.11	% Hispanic	0.00	.00
Party control	0.01	.04	% Asian	0.01*	.00
Size of district	0.00*	.00	% Democratic	0.00	.00
Size of chamber	0.00*	.00	% college educated	0.01*	.00
South	-0.27	.06	% age 55 and over	-0.01	.00
District safeness	0.00	.00	% farm sector	-0.01*	.00
Legislator's party	0.05	.05	% service sector	0.00	.00
Tenure	-0.02	.01	% government sector	-0.01	.01
			Avg. Household inc.	0.00	.00
N = 2,204 Adj. R^2 = .17					

Source: 1995 Survey of State Legislators.

*$p < .05$

** Difference between NCTLs and NCNTLs: p = .06 (one-tailed)

The survey results with respect to time budgets suggest significant differences between legislators' relationships with constituents in term-limit and non-term-limit states, differences that warranted follow-up in our interviews. When we asked interview subjects whether term limits had any effect on the relationship between legislators and constituents, the responses varied. The principal division was between those from Maine,

TABLE 3.6. Time Spent on Pork by Old and New State Legislators in Term-Limit and Non-Term-Limit States

Dependent variable:			Making sure district gets fair share of government money and projects		
Scale:			A great deal = 1, to Hardly any = 5		
Residual group:			OTNTL		
Legislative group			b	Standard error	
OTTL			.25*	.06	
NCNTL			-.17*	.08	
NCTL**			.31*	.10	
Control Variables	b	s.e.		b	s.e.
Constant	2.83*	.37	District characteristics		
Chamber	-0.12	.07	% Black	0.00	.00
Professionalization	-0.92*	.13	% Hispanic	0.00	.00
Party control	0.02	.06	% Asian	0.01*	.00
Size of district	0.00	.00	% Democratic	-0.01*	.00
Size of chamber	0.00	.00	% college educated	0.01*	.00
South	-0.20*	.07	% age 55 and over	-0.01*	.00
District safeness	0.00*	.00	% farm sector	-0.01	.00
Legislator's party	0.37*	.15	% service sector	0.01	.00
Tenure	-0.05*	.02	% government sector	-0.01	.01
			Avg. Household inc.	0.00	.00
N = 2,204 Adj. R^2 = .17					

Source: 1995 Survey of State Legislators.

* $p < .05$

** Difference between NCTLs and NCNTLs: $p < .01$

where the ratio of constituents to legislators is unusually small, and those in states where district population is larger and the relationship with constituents less personal. The consistent account from Maine is that small districts guarantee that legislators will be held accountable to constituents regardless of the prospects for reelection. As Dan Gwadosky (D-ME), a former Speaker of the House, put it,

> Our districts in Maine are very small compared to the nation, and so most of our representatives have a pretty strong identification with their districts. In the House we're representing about 8,400 people, so you see their constituents at the football game or at the supermarket. You used to see them at the dump; now we see them at the transfer station. You know them by first name, in many circumstances, and you know your constituents well. I don't think that that will change necessarily. We haven't seen a change.

Jim Donnelly (R-ME) concurred:

> We have a big enough legislature for a small enough state that really the constituency you're dealing with is pretty much your friends and neighbors, so it's not a very anonymous system. So if you decide to ignore your neighbor, you'll hear about it at the grocery store. So I don't think term limits [are] going to make you exempt from the pressures.

The ratio of citizens to legislators is far lower in Maine, however, than the national average.[5] In our three other interview states, legislators were far more prone to indicate that term limits affected relationships with constituents. House Majority Leader Barbara Lisk (R-WA) said,

> I have noticed a subtle difference in my constituents, what they expect of my future. There's a real subtle inference now in most meetings I go to that I will be running for the Senate in the next elections because I'm term-limited in the House. And it looks like I have a senator that will be retiring—he's elderly and has somewhat indicated to me [that he will not] run again. The inference from my constituency is almost automatic now wherever I go that I'm running for Senate—and I have made no announcement. Actually, I haven't made any plans to do that. It's an interesting situation for me anyway.

Lisk's answer focuses exclusively on her constituents' expectations of her career aspirations without explicitly addressing whether term limits alter legislator behavior. Senator Johnston suggests a more straightforward effect of term limits in loosening the constituent-legislator bond by reducing the incentives for legislators to interact with those they represent: "I go to fewer social events than I used to now that I cannot be reelected." Representative Thomas suggests that by mandating an end date on the representative-constituent relationship, term limits provide some slack to allow greater independence from constituents' demands:

> Before, if a constituent said something I disagreed with, I might tend to soft-pedal. Now, I'm much more likely to tell them, "I think you're simply wrong." In that sense, you might say there's been some improvement.

Thomas's comment nicely sums up what has been one of the main points of controversy in the popular debate over term limits. Some proponents argue that limits will encourage legislatures to address politically difficult issues that may require policy solutions with unpalatable short-term effects (Will 1992), whereas many opponents argue that limits will undermine the responsiveness and accountability of elected officials. Thomas's comment suggests that both sides are correct, and he regards the increased independence from constituent pressure favorably. As usual with term limits, others who agreed on the basic premise reached the opposite judgment. Said Finneran,

> I think it would be a risk, not only in being somewhat less responsive to constituent issues or concerns, but I think that there's a risk that you might attract some rascals who are just determined to plunder or attempt to enrich themselves. . . . Then it's wide open—it's like the wild, wild West!

As for any effects on the tendency of legislators to pursue narrow district interests, perhaps to the detriment of broader concerns, the interview data are more ambiguous than the surveys. Senator Alpert suggested that term limits encourage narrow regionalism by eliminating long-term relationships that make cooperation on broader policy issues possible:

> *Alpert:* I think people are actually more parochial because they are looking at things for such a short time frame that there's very little long-term vision. . . . The greater good for the greater number kind of thing, I think, is when you look at things long term, but when you're only there for such a short period of time, you often are just more parochial in your interest, I think.

Interviewer: Any specific examples of that come to mind?

Alpert: Well, actually, we're struggling with a bridge retrofit issue here in California on toll bridges that need to be retrofitted for potential future earthquakes in the state. This is one that appears to be—most of the toll bridges are in the northern part of the state, so there seems to be an issue that is just breaking down on geographical lines—and it doesn't seem that there's anybody standing back and saying, "This is the entire state of California. Let's think about what's best for the whole state of California."

Interviewer: Do you think this would have played out differently prior to the term limits?

Alpert: I don't know. But I sure don't think, you know, that term limits has made it any better.[6]

Alpert's suggestion is interesting in part because it turns the traditional political science logic behind pork-barrel politics on its head, suggesting that reelection is not the main motivation behind district provincialism but that vote trading among legislators over prolonged periods sustains cooperation in the provision of public goods rather than particularistic logrolling.

Alpert's suggestion aside, however, additional items from the survey data support the suggestion that term limits loosen the tie between legislators and their districts. We asked legislators two survey questions specifically to address this issue: first, whether they should be primarily concerned with the needs of their district or the state as a whole (district = 1 to state as whole = 7); and second, whether they should follow the demands of district voters or their own conscience if the two should conflict (always district = 1 to always conscience = 7). On neither question is there a significant difference between OTNTLs and OTTLs or between these groups and NCTLs. But NCNTLs were more inclined toward district demands than any of these groups on both questions (see tables 3.7 and 3.8).

These results might be interpreted a number of ways. First, they are consistent with the position, reviewed previously, that term limits dampen the responsiveness of legislators to their constituents (Zupan 1990; Carey 1994). Second, the results suggest that term limits encourage precisely the sort of detachment from the demands of narrow district interests that Burkeans like George Will (1992) propound. Indeed, even some interviewees who unambiguously opposed term limits on other grounds found the Burkean ideal both appealing and relevant. As former Assemblyman Joseph Mayo (D-ME) described it,

Mayo: The mind-set and the attitude of a member does change significantly when they know they're no longer going to be here. I experienced that myself. . . . When a member has decided not to seek reelection, they tend to be a little bit more relaxed. They don't tend to be as concerned about the winds of what the public is screaming about. . . . They seem to be a bit freer.

TABLE 3.7.   Responsiveness to State versus District Interests of Old and New State Legislators in Term-Limit and Non-Term-Limit States

Dependent variable:			Look after needs of district versus state as a whole		
Scale:			District = 1, to State as whole = 7		
Residual group:			OTNTL		
Legislative group			b	Standard error	
OTTL			.03	.09	
NCNTL			-.28*	.12	
NCTL**			.08	.14	
Control Variables	b	s.e.		b	s.e.
Constant	3.47*	.54	District characteristics		
Chamber	0.22*	.11	% Black	-0.00	.00
Professionalization	-1.24*	.20	% Hispanic	0.01	.00
Party control	0.13	.08	% Asian	0.02*	.01
Size of district	0.00	.00	% Democratic	-0.01*	.00
Size of chamber	0.00*	.00	% college educated	0.02*	.01
South	-0.05	.10	% age 55 and over	0.00	.01
District safeness	-0.00	.00	% farm sector	-0.01	.01
Legislator's party	0.02	.09	% service sector	0.01	.01
Tenure	0.02	.02	% government sector	0.00	.02
			Avg. Household inc.	0.00	.00
N = 2,211 Adj. R^2 = .07					

Source: 1995 Survey of State Legislators.

*$p < .05$

** Difference between NCTLs and NCNTLs: $p = .01$

Interviewer: Is that an argument in favor of term limits?
Mayo: Oh yeah, I think it is. I think it is, yeah! There aren't very many good arguments for term limits, but that might be one of them.

There is some irony, however, in that although newcomers in term-limit states appear to be less beholden to narrow district interests than are new-

TABLE 3.8.   Responsiveness to Conscience versus District Interests of Old and New State Legislators in Term-Limit and Non-Term-Limit States

Dependent variable:			Follow conscience or demands of district when there is a conflict between the two		
Scale:			Always district = 1, to Always conscience = 7		
Residual group:			OTNTL		
Legislative group			b	Standard error	
OTTL			.03	.09	
NCNTL			-.13	.12	
NCTL**			.13	.14	
Control Variables	b	s.e.		b	s.e.
Constant	4.00*	.53	District characteristics		
Chamber	0.17	.10	% Black	0.00	.00
Professionalization	-0.51*	.19	% Hispanic	0.00	.00
Party control	0.00	.08	% Asian	0.01	.00
Size of district	0.00*	.00	% Democratic	0.00	.00
Size of chamber	0.00*	.00	% college educated	0.02	.01
South	-0.23*	.10	% age 55 and over	0.01	.01
District safeness	0.00	.00	% farm sector	-0.02*	.01
Legislator's party	-0.19*	.09	% service sector	0.00	.01
Tenure	0.03	.02	% government sector	0.02	.01
			Avg. Household inc.	0.00	.00
N = 2,197 Adj. R^2 = .05					

Source: 1995 Survey of State Legislators.

** Difference between NCTLs and NCNTLs: p = .06

comers in non-term-limit states, newcomers are indistinguishable on these counts from old-timers in both term-limit and non-term-limit states. Perhaps Burkean detachment can be encouraged as easily through long tenure and incumbency advantage as through term limits.

A third theme related to reelection-related activities and the severing of district connections concerns legislators' commitment to their current positions and the effect of the search for postlegislative office or employment. Among our survey respondents, the significant point is that when we asked them whether they regarded public office as a career, term limits have no impact—among either cohort—on the likelihood of an affirmative answer. The existence of term limits also does not appear to have much impact on whether legislators treat their elected office as a profession. Term-limited legislators are no more likely than nonlimited ones to hold jobs outside the legislature, suggesting that the citizen-legislator ideal of retaining strong links to one's private station is not realized.

Consistent with these results was the conviction among interview respondents from all four states that maneuvering for postlegislative posts becomes a dominant concern for term-limited legislators. The most conventional career trajectory for state legislators leads either through state senates or to Congress, as the anonymous California assembly member described:

> I think a lot of people thought [term limits were] going to bring in your basic citizen-legislator who was going to want to serve for a couple terms and then go back to whatever he was doing before—and that's just completely wrong. Most people walk in and the first day they walk in the door they can tell you what Senate seat they're running for, "Because I'm nested with a guy whose Senate seat is expiring in *this* year, because I'll have a leg up because my opponent on the other side represents fewer voters than I do and I'm going to be in better shape than he is," or "I'm going to go to Congress in *this* year." Look, people who want to do this kind of stuff are professionally oriented and want to make it a profession.

The interviews, however, also turned up ideas about postlegislative aspirations in the term-limit environment that were less conventional. Assemblyman Thomas said,

> A lot of people are leaving for city and county positions, because they pay—especially county offices. They're full time, they pay a lot better than what we get here, and they don't have term limits.

Thomas's response suggests that term limits may alter the traditional trajectory of local to state to national government. State legislators, who now face a larger pack of experienced competitors looking to move up to statewide office or to the U.S. Congress, might consider municipal and county jobs that have less prestige but allow one to sustain a political career. Senate President Lockyer likewise sees term limits encouraging job searches among alternative careers but is more pessimistic about the implications:

> *Lockyer:* Before [term limits], the bulk of [senators] would have been happy to continue to serve in the Senate for the foreseeable future. Some always did—and more now do—look at statewide office. A few look at going back to the Assembly. Some are preparing to retire, but not many. Some want to lobby or other things. One of the distressing things you see is when a chair—and this goes back to the Assembly, not our chamber—but a chairman of a powerful committee, a year and a half ahead of departure due to term limits, is meeting with the executives of that industry to try to secure employment for when the term ends. That kind of thing is bothersome.
>
> *Interviewer:* Is that something that is fairly widespread?
>
> *Lockyer:* No. But it's happened. Mostly, probably, they don't tell.

Conclusion

Our results on the effects of term limits on the behavior of individual legislators, both within the survey and between the survey and interviews, are mixed. The interviews suggest that term limits encourage legislative showboating and taking of positions and undermine legislative cooperation based on long-term relationships of mutual compromise and exchange. The survey data turn up no term-limit effects on legislators' reported efforts at coalition-building or studying legislation, but the data do indicate that term limits encourage legislative newcomers to be more active in proposing new legislation. This result is consistent with the tenor of the interviews, though senior legislators were generally unimpressed with the newcomers' proposals.

The surveys also indicate that term limits are associated with less-district-oriented electioneering activities, even while showing that newcomers in term-limit states are as committed to their political careers as their counterparts in non-term-limit states. One interpretation of this difference is that term limits encourage a sort of Burkean detachment from narrow district concerns and, correspondingly, perhaps, a greater attention to the good of the state as a whole. Most of our interview subjects were more skeptical, emphasizing the efforts of term-limited legislators to position themselves either for postlegislative office with a different constituency or for other postlegislative employment connected to their current political performance. The effects of term limits on legislative behavior discussed in this chapter are summarized in table 3.9.

TABLE 3.9.   Summary Effects of Term Limits on Legislators' Behavior and Priorities

Projected Effect on	Detected Effect of Term Limits	Evidence
Cooperation	undermine long-term relationships built on trust	legislator interviews
Individualism	encourage position-taking, seeking spotlight to build personal reputation	legislator interviews
Coalition-building	none	1995 survey data
New legislation	encourage newcomers to propose more policy initiatives	1995 survey data and legislator interviews
Quality of legislation	reduce effort developing policy expertise; undermine quality of proposals	legislator interviews
Pork barreling	declines	1995 survey data
District orientation	increase relevance of statewide concerns, demands of conscience, relative to district demands	1995 survey data and legislator interviews
Reelection intentions	decline among old timers; no effect on newcomers	1995 survey data
Campaigning, fundraising	reduce efforts by old timers	1995 survey data
Political careerism	none	1995 survey data and legislator interviews
Constituent relationships	reduce contact with constituents and casework; decrease relevance of pressure from constituents—at least in states with high constituent to legislator ratios	1995 survey data and legislator interviews

From the perspective of the amount of change associated with the term-limit reform, the results in this chapter suggest greater effects than were observed for the composition of the legislature. Whereas in chapter 2 we found little change attributable to term limits in the demographic and ideological characteristics of legislators, here we found a number of effects that are consistent with one another and seem to have a direct connection with the changing incentives that accompany a term-limit regime. The differences were not dramatic—we did not see radical alterations in legislators' perspectives: many remain motivated by political careerism, even if that desire now causes them to behave slightly differently. Moreover, the differences sometimes suggested cross-cutting results, as when term-limited legislators appear to be more concerned with legislation but may simultaneously be more concerned with finding a postlegislative job. In any event, as we turn from demographics to legislator behavior, we begin to see how term limits can quickly alter the legislative scene. We shall see still more changes as we move on to consider the legislature as an institution.

CHAPTER 4

Institutional Effects

The expectations of political scientists and activists regarding institutional effects of term limits vary more than in any other area. There are predictions that term limits will increase the power of party leaders because parties will gain increased control over candidate recruitment (Brady and Rivers 1991) and arguments that the reform will decrease the authority of party leaders because their control over legislative committee assignments will mean little to term-limited legislators (Malbin and Benjamin 1992). Similarly, some argue that limits will decrease the influence of lobbyists as legislators ineligible for reelection will be uninterested in the campaign contributions of interest groups (Mitchell 1991), while others contend that lame-duck legislators will curry favor with corporations and interest groups in exchange for postlegislative employment (Cohen and Spitzer 1996). Some suggest that by undermining legislative competence, term limits will increase the power of governors (Grofman and Sutherland 1996), whereas others hold that term limits will fortify the deliberative independence of legislatures vis-à-vis the executive (Will 1992).

We began with slighter expectations of detecting institutional change than of measuring change in either legislative composition or behavior, on the grounds that changes in the influence of various institutional actors might take longer to manifest themselves than would effects on composition and behavior. Changes in the procedural powers of committees or party leaders, for example, may require rewriting the rules governing organization of the legislature, which may not be feasible until the legislature has been largely renewed under the term-limits regime.[1] Contrary to this expectation, however, both our survey and interview results indicate substantial institutional changes as a result of term limits. In fact, our data suggest that institutional changes in the early years of term limits are more substantial than changes in either legislative composition or behavior. The institutional effects of term limits picked up by our surveys and elaborated on by our interview subjects, moreover, reflect directly on many issues at the heart of the term-limits debate.

In looking for institutional effects, the analysis is simplified in some respects because appropriate comparisons are more straightforward than in the previous two chapters. In asking survey questions about the relative power of various institutional actors, unlike questions on personal characteristics or behavior, we regard the judgments of all members of a legislature to be comparable, regardless of whether they were elected before or after term limits were adopted. Thus, we distinguish between legislators in term-limit and non-term-limit states but not between old-timers and newcomers. However, those best able to assess the power of various political actors should be those who have served long enough to have perspective on the organization and performance of the institution. Thus, we draw only on the survey responses of nonfreshman legislators.[2]

Institutional changes are complex phenomena, the motivations and mechanics of which warrant more detailed explanation than is generally compatible with our survey's short-answer or multiple-choice format. For this reason, we relied on the survey primarily for an overall sense of how legislators perceive the relative powers of various actors in state politics and whether the balance of powers among these actors is changing. We used that initial information to construct open-ended questions that prompted our interview subjects to elaborate on the nature of institutional change. The survey data with respect to institutional change are drawn from two batteries of questions. For expositional simplicity, we present these results in their entirety first and then move on to the interview results.

Survey Results

The first battery of survey questions asked respondents to rate the influence of various actors and institutions on legislative outcomes along a seven-point scale, from "no influence" (1) to "dictates policy" (7). These responses allow for cross-sectional analysis of whether term-limit states differ from non-term-limit states in the balance of policy-making influence among institutional actors. The second battery of questions asked respondents to rate any changes in the influence of the same list of actors over the past two to three years (roughly since the adoption of term limits in term-limit states) on a five-point scale from "big decrease" (1) to "big increase" (5), with "no change" (3) at the middle of the scale. The actors listed were:

- majority party leadership
- minority party leadership
- committee chairs
- governor
- legislative staff
- bureaucrats/civil servants

- interest groups
- mass media

As in previous chapters, the results are in the form of regression equations in which we include control variables for the characteristics of the respondents and the legislative chambers in which they serve. Here, however, the comparisons are much simpler than in previous chapters in that there are only two comparison groups—legislators in non-term-limit states and in term-limit states. Since one group is always compared against the other, we have to represent only the difference—that is, a single number. In turn, the fact that we can represent each regression by a single number means that we can show the results of a number of regressions in a single table. Indeed, results for all of the institutional actors listed are shown in table 4.1. The entry in the first row (–.16) represents the estimated effect of term limits on the perceived influence of majority party leadership, the entry in the second row shows the presumed effect of term limits on minority party leadership, and so on.[3]

With respect to the overall influence of the various actors, the results in table 4.1 indicate important differences across the two types of states. Legislators in term-limit states rate the influence of the majority party leadership significantly lower than those in non-term-limit states. The influence of committee chairs is rated the same in both groups. The influence of all other actors is considered higher in term-limit states than in non-term-limit states, with the greatest differences for the governor and the mass media. With the exception of the coefficient for minority party leadership (which is not statistically significant), these results are consistent with arguments that term limits weaken legislators relative to other actors involved in policy-making. Opponents of term limits contend that the reforms should augment the power of legislative staff, civil servants, and interest groups at the expense of legislators. The relevant coefficients in table 4.1 are consistent with these arguments, but they also are not statistically significant. It may be that the influence lost by elected legislators is being widely and unevenly redistributed, with the governor gaining most. Alternatively, these early results may not be indicative of the full redistribution of power that will eventually result from the adoption of term limits. Our interview responses shed more light on these issues.

The second battery of questions—regarding changes in influence during the first few years after term limits were adopted in those states that have them—allows us to develop this picture further by directly addressing the issue of change over time. The survey responses here are not time-series data. Ideally, we would have a series of responses to the first battery of questions from across an extended time period, which would allow us to

TABLE 4.1. Perceived Influence of Institutional Actors on Legislative Outcomes

Dependent variable:	Various institutional actors affected by term limits[a]	
Scale:	No influence = 1, to Dictates policy = 7	
Residual category:	Non-term-limit states	
Institutional actors	b	Standard error
Majority party leadership	-.16*	.08
Minority party leadership	.09	.07
Committee chairs	-.01	.07
Governor	.15*	.08
Legislative staff	.08	.08
Bureaucrats/civil service	.08	.07
Interest groups	.05	.07
Mass media	.15*	.08
$N \approx 1,570$		

Source: 1995 Survey of State Legislators.

Note: Each *b* indicates the difference between the responses of legislators in term-limit-states and in non-term-limit states (the residual category). That is, the *b*'s represent the effect of term limits on the perceived influence of each actor. A positive coefficient indicates that legislators in TL states judged the actor as having more influence over policy. Results are based on responses from legislators serving their second term or more.

[a] For each dependent variable, we used the same controls as in the regressions in chapters 2 and 3. How many and which coefficients are significant vary from one equation to another. The average adjusted $R^2 = .04$.

*$p < .05$

identify any patterns in legislators' perceptions of the current power balance. Repeating our survey longer after the adoption and implementation of term limits will, we hope, eventually allow us to collect such data. For now, with one survey, we tried to approximate such an effect by asking legislators about their perceptions of changes in relative powers.

The results are consistent with the evaluations of overall influence on policy from the first battery of questions (see table 4.2). Majority party leaders are perceived by legislators in term-limit states as having suffered a loss of influence in recent years relative to their counterparts in non-term-limit states (or, alternatively, they have gained less power than majority party leaders in NTL states).[4] This finding provides stronger evidence for the decline of influence of majority party leaders than the first questions because it is much less plausible that changes could be attributed to differences between term-limit and non-term-limit states prior to the adoption of term limits that are not captured by our control variables.

The coefficients for three actors—mass media, committee chairs, and interest groups—are virtually zero. The adoption of limits themselves thus does not appear to account for the difference between term-limit and non-term-limit states in the perceived influence of the mass media. The absence of a perceived effect on committee chairs and interest groups runs somewhat counter to much of our interview data; as discussed in the following section, committee chairs are regarded, on balance, as having lost influence and interest groups are regarded as having gained influence. A plausible explanation for this discrepancy is the relative timing of our survey and interviews: at the time of the surveys, term limits had not gone into effect in any states, whereas at the time of the interviews, term limits had already removed their first cohort of legislators in Maine and California. Moreover, interview respondents in these states report the biggest changes in the influence of committee chairs and interest groups. Conversely, there is competing commentary in some of the interviews suggesting that countervailing factors strengthen chairs and weaken interest groups. We subsequently discuss these issues at greater length.

The strongest positive result from the surveys is in agreement between the two batteries of items: governors gained the most at the expense of the power of the majority party leadership. We also find that legislative staffs were reported to have gained power under the adoption of term limits. This result, although statistically significant, is not suggested by the previous battery, so it should be viewed more cautiously. One other key actor, the bureaucracy or civil service, shows more influence in term-limit states than in non-term-limit states for both batteries of items, although the differences fall short of statistical significance.

TABLE 4.2.   Changes over the Past Two to Three Years in the Influence of Various Institutional Actors on Legislative Outcomes

Dependent variables:	Various institutional actors affected by term limits[a]	
Scale:	Big decrease = 1 to Big increase = 5	
Residual category:	Non-term-limit states	
Institutional actors	b	Standard error
Majority party leadership	-.18*	.06
Minority party leadership	.03	.06
Committee chairs	-.01	.04
Governor	.16*	.06
Legislative staff	.09*	.03
Bureaucrats/civil service	.05	.03
Interest groups	-.01	.04
Mass media	-.01	.04
$N=1,540$		

Source: 1995 Survey of State Legislators.

Note: Each *b* indicates the difference between the responses of legislators in term limit states and the responses of legislators in non-term limit states (the residual category). That is, the *b*'s represent the effect of term limits on changes in the perceived influence of each actor. A positive coefficient indicates that legislators in TL states judged the actor as having increased its influence over policy. Results are based on responses from legislators serving their second term or more.

[a] For each dependent variable, we used the same controls as in the regressions in chapters 2 and 3. How many and which coefficients are significant vary from one equation to another. The average adjusted $R^2 = .04$.

* $p < .05$

Interview Results

The interview data on institutional effects of term limits are rich. With respect to the survey results that are strongest and most unambiguous—regarding effects on executives and legislative party leaders—the interviews support and flesh out the mechanics of the changes. With regard to the more ambiguous survey results, particularly on committees, the interviews provide insights into the motivations of legislators and the operation of legislatures that the blunt instrument of a survey could not have detected. The less-structured format of the interviews also provides unforeseen intuitions regarding the effects of term limits on legislative organization and the possibility of cooperation between upper and lower chambers of state legislatures. We address these issues in turn.

Effects on Executive Influence

As with the surveys, the overwhelming conclusion among interview subjects was that term limits increase the executive branch's policy influence relative to the legislature. Brian Lees (R-MA) mitigated this verdict somewhat on the grounds that more professionalized legislatures, with greater institutional resources, would be weakened less than those where service is a part-time proposition and staffing is meager. Nevertheless, consensus on increased executive authority was strong. The most common rationale was that executives have greater access to and control over the informational and technical expertise of the state government bureaucracy. Thus, even though governors themselves are subject to term limits in thirty-nine states (Stanley and Niemi 1998, 291–93), they will be able to command technical expertise quickly and effectively, whereas novice legislators under term limits will negotiate with the executive under a widening informational disadvantage (Finneran, D-MA). The perception of resource asymmetry is provided by former representative and current House Clerk Joseph Mayo (D-ME):

> When Maine became a state, in 1820, the governor was relatively weak; the legislature was very strong. It's the direct opposite now. The legislature is relatively weak compared to the governor. The governor has the forces of 10,000 state employees behind him. We have a part-time citizen legislature with 130 employees.

Maine's Senate president, Democrat Mark Lawrence, laid out the effects of this situation:

I think [term limits] increase the power of the governor with the legislature because you have so many new people, and information is power, and the executive has so much more information than the legislature does—with so many people who don't know the history of what's going on with government. It makes it easier for a governor to protect certain parts of the bureaucracy that they want to protect and eliminate some that they may want to eliminate.

Majority leader Chelly Pingree (D-ME) concurred:

[Governors are advantaged] especially in a state where [governors] have four-year terms and the potential for longer terms. Governors can get up to speed much more quickly and have bigger staffs. Yes, I think it gives power to the executive branch.

This informational asymmetry was the most common explanation for increased executive power, but another account, also based on the governor's control over the bureaucracy, warrants mention. The president of the California Senate, Democrat Bill Lockyer, emphasized executives' control of coveted postlegislative appointments as a source of influence over incumbent lawmakers:

[The governor's influence has increased] in terms of potential employment. Those legislators that are of the same political party as the governor might be a little more cautious about doing things that the governor disapproves of than they used to be. An extraordinary number of them in our state have gone to work, or they are appointed to things, by Pete Wilson, if they were okay people—okay Republicans.

This account is particularly noteworthy in comparison to the effects of term limits in comparative perspective. In research on Costa Rica, the one democracy to have imposed legislative term limits for an extended period, Carey (1996) found that a principal effect is to generate dependence among ambitious legislators on future presidents, who control access to key appointed posts during the period immediately after the current legislative term. In Costa Rica, because the terms and term limits on presidents and legislators are concurrent, the identity of the president who will control coveted appointments for incumbent legislators is unknown throughout most of the legislative term. At the state level in the United States, however, longer terms (four years for most governors, two years for most lower chambers) and staggered terms (in many upper chambers) mean that incumbent governors, even when term-limited, will certainly control appointment prospects for some term-limited legislators. This situation suggests, as does Lockyer's comment, that the increased influence of governors over legislators through appointments could be substantial.

Effects on Legislative Party Leaders

Agreement among interview respondents that term limits weaken the authority of legislative party leaders over rank-and-file legislators was as consistent as agreement about strengthened executives. The expected effect of term limits on the influence of party leaders is based on standard models of legislative organization, which emphasize the authority delegated to party leaders to control resources valuable to legislators who aspire to reelection (Rohde 1991; Cox and McCubbins 1993). By these accounts, party leaders exercise influence over policy largely by inducing cohesiveness within their party caucuses and by putting together coalitions behind policy. They marshal such support through the distribution to rank-and-file legislators of such "goods" as committee assignments, privileged procedural status for legislation, staff and office support, and publicity and fund-raising assistance for campaigns.

Term limits could be expected to affect the relationship between party leaders and their caucuses in a couple of ways. First, if the resources controlled by party leaders decreased in importance to the rank and file, then leadership's ability to enforce party discipline should decline. For example, if committee assignments became less relevant to legislators who are legally prohibited from building careers within a given chamber, then the currency legislative party leaders use to purchase support for their initiatives should decline in value.[5] Second, term limits may upset the equilibrium between leaders and the rank and file by curtailing the time period over which leaders can compensate legislators for their support or punish those who buck leadership directives. If promises of future favors from party leaders are worthless to term-limited legislators, not only will leaders have less ability to elicit support, but they may face an increased threat of insurrection if they attempt to exercise leadership prerogatives in the short run.

The description of Senate Minority Leader Lees of the value of committee assignments suggests some support for the first scenario:

> I think some people used to think that if you got on some committee, you ought to stay there, you could make a name for yourself, you could do something, potentially even go onto another job from there.

Where now, people don't think that way. They think "I ought to try a couple of committees." . . . Now, you've got eight years. Do it or get out, especially if you get some non–high profile committee. You don't want to stay there long, even if it's an important committee.

Lees's account is ambiguous, however. He implies that although any particular committee assignment might be less valuable to legislators with short time horizons, the ability to secure new committee assignments without long waiting periods is more valuable. As a result, to the extent that party leaders control committee assignments, the value of this currency could rise under term limits. This account is supported by Representative Brian Thomas (R-WA) and also by Lees's colleague across the aisle, Senator Stanley Rosenberg (D-MA):

> *Interviewer:* Are positions on particular committees or are chairmanships as important to individual legislators as they were before term limits?
>
> *Rosenberg:* Absolutely! Absolutely! . . . Because you know you're going to be here a shorter period of time and because you're desperate to get the committee assignment, why wouldn't you be more cooperative rather than less and think, "What would I do and how much would I give up, if I really wanted to be the chair of Committee X?" I would think, if I were going to make a career of it and I knew I could be here twenty or thirty years, I might behave differently and be a little more independent, if I needed to be, for my district or my own principles or conscience. . . . With term limits, I might pay more attention, because there would be fewer Speakers and fewer opportunities to be chosen by a Speaker under term limits than if I could make a career of it here and [I could] wait out a Speaker that I didn't agree with.

In Maine's less-professionalized legislature, the marginal increase in access to staff and the resources associated with chairmanships plays a relatively larger role in respondents' rationales, as illustrated by Senator Pingree:

> I think there's a lot of prestige around being a committee chair. You're usually the spokesperson, which all politicians want to be in the press. In an understaffed legislature like ours, they're the only people with staff. Rank and file in our legislature don't have offices or staff. Committee chairs have clerks and offices. Besides being in leadership itself, they're the only thing people fight for around here. That is the biggest power of the presiding officer is to have those things.

In this light, the second scenario appears to be more convincing than the first in accounting for any decline in the authority of legislative party leaders. It is not that the resources they control are less valuable but that the period for which they control them—and for which these resources are relevant to rank-and-file legislators—is compressed. If anything, the demand for choice committee assignments appears to be higher under term limits, but the ability of the leadership to meet this demand to the satisfaction of legislators is compromised. As Senate President Lockyer put it,

> People will get more aggressive about trying to pick up a chairmanship that they want, because they know they are only going to be there a short amount of time—not being patient when somebody is already there, that sort of thing. It creates a little more friction.

The legislators we interviewed, both inside and outside formal leadership positions in their parties, regarded the fact that there is a known end point to legislative careers as undermining their authority. Comments along these lines ranged from the speculative to the cataclysmic. Maine party leaders exhibited typical Yankee reserve. Said House Majority Leader Carol Kontos, a Democrat,

> I'm termed out, so I'm a lame duck right now. . . . And so, as somebody pointed out, you're already, you're quickly irrelevant in terms of how the caucus sees you, because they don't need your good will for next session.

Echoed Republican House Minority Leader Jim Donnelly,

> I'm a lame-duck leader just like the Speaker is. I'm in my fourth term. So it's going to be interesting.

Massachusetts House Speaker Thomas Finneran, a Democrat, more explicitly described the calculation confronted by both leaders and led:

> [Term limits] affect my ability to [put together coalitions] because if somebody is operating on this now artificially imposed deadline, they're looking to either move to higher office or another office because the calendar is marching against them. They are then very, very much less likely to abide by any type of committee assignments that I make, the delegation of committee responsibilities, with a suggestion to those who have only been here a little while, "You have to wait your turn. You have to develop a little seasoning, a little bit of

experience," and the like. There could be, quite frankly, an incipient revolution, I think, at any point in any legislature that has term limits from those who are not part of the leadership. There's no gain for them to wait because when they wait, the guillotine falls on their head.

This opinion was shared by legislators outside the party leadership structure as well. House Finance Committee Chair Thomas said,

> *Thomas:* People come in here in their first term, and they've made too many promises. They think they're going to change the world, they don't understand how things work, they don't understand what it means to work together. The leadership can't tell them what to do. In their second term, they understand a little more about how things get done, but just enough to be dangerous.
> *Interviewer:* So you think parties will be less cohesive under term limits?
> *Thomas:* No comparison. It'll be chaos.

The consensus on this issue and the forcefulness with which some legislators expressed their opinion on it warrant reviewing another example at length. One member of the California Assembly, understandably requesting anonymity, stated,

> *Legislator:* I think that now party leaders and party discipline mean nothing. There isn't any such thing. So the party breakdown is severe. And even within a caucus, what are supposed to be the organizationally empowered individuals, well. . . . You know no one would ever dare cross [the former House Speaker]—you just didn't do it. But people feel pretty free to cross the new ranks of leadership. And right now I can tell you that if our governor and the president of the Senate and the Speaker of the Assembly and their Republican counterparts—the four highest-ranking legislators and the governor—sat down and cut a deal and said "This is what we're going to do on taxes this year," the rest of us don't have to go along with it. I can feel free to say "To hell with you guys. I don't have to support that deal." I don't owe it to my Speaker. I don't owe it to the governor. I don't owe it to anybody. People can become much more sort of single-issue focused, and if all I care about is abortion funding, I don't care if the governor is telling me "I can't get your pet thing in there but just be patient," I'll just vote no and tell him to go look for some votes somewhere else.

Interviewer: Are there specific sanctions that the leadership used to exercise that they don't exercise anymore because of term limits?

Legislator: Absolutely. I think the leadership is afraid to even make demands because they know they can't back up the demands. But the sanctions that used to be imposed could include everything from lack of financial support in your next campaign to withholding key committee assignments, from loss of your staff, of the quality of office that you occupy—all that kind of stuff. The leadership just wouldn't dare play those kinds of games anymore. The Speaker needs your support to keep this job, in which he has diminished power, and he can only keep it if we let him keep it. And since there's plenty of other people willing to undermine him, to take the job away from him, he really can't afford to alienate anyone.

The common theme in these statements is that the authority of party leaders is based on being able to commit credibly to future payoffs or sanctions to rank-and-file legislators in exchange for current concessions and that such commitment is destabilized when there is a fixed and known end point on tenure (of both leaders and rank and file) associated with term limits. The argument is consistent across legislators both inside and outside the formal leadership structures of their parties. It is worth noting, however, that destabilizing the exchange relationship between leaders and led could conceivably cut two ways—it might undermine the willingness of the rank and file to accede to leadership demands, but it might also encourage leaders to defect on established norms under which legislators are generally rewarded for party loyalty. In only one instance did a party leader we interviewed suggest such a scenario. Speaker Finneran contended,

[Term limits] changed the way I looked at some things when I made my first series of [committee] appointments in April. I was elected Speaker in April, and I made some new appointments, changed some assignments around here in May. I thought it was important to break away from just purely seniority and a couple of other traditional approaches to committee assignments that I think, for all intents and purposes, cluttered it with people who had length of service. I'm a believer in promoting talent, and I believe in promoting it quickly. That belief was, perhaps, strengthened by this advent of term limits. Once upon a time, it would not have been so difficult for me or inappropriate for any other Speaker to say to somebody who shows talent, "Be patient with me. Another term or two and I'll be able to move you into the hierarchy of things." A term or two now and that's literally the end of their career, so it would be entirely fair for them to look me right in the eye and fix my gaze and say, "You're asking me to wait until the death sentence is imposed. I can't do that, and I won't do that." So, for me, there's been a direct and an immediate impact on my determination to move those people up.

As with many arguments surrounding term limits, Finneran's account suggests subtly different potential effects. In one sense, his case that term limits have liberated him to make committee assignments on the basis of talent rather than seniority resonates with reform advocates' claims that term limits will increase policy innovation and break policy gridlock. Skeptics, conversely, might counter that a party leader's judgment of what constitutes "talent" may be controversial and that Finneran's case here is simply a veiled argument for increased leadership discretion to make assignments by unspecified criteria. In turn, the argument that term limits increase the authority of party leaders is contradicted by our survey data and by all our interview responses, with the exception of this one passage from Finneran. Indeed, Finneran himself appears ambiguous on this point (as his earlier statements indicate). In the two passages quoted in this chapter, he lays out a case that term limits freed him to break seniority norms but also a competing case that, under term limits, a leader who fails to comply quickly with the demands of his copartisans faces an increased risk of revolt within the caucus.

Finneran may be correct on both points. By all accounts, term limits destabilize the exchange relationship between leaders and rank-and-file legislators. In the short run, this situation may encourage leaders to care less about maintaining support within the caucus and to take actions unpopular among their copartisans in pursuit of legislative goals. Term limits may also encourage the rank and file to ignore leadership directives on the grounds that future compensation is uncertain or irrelevant or even to replace leaders who are not sufficiently responsive in the short run to the demands of their caucus members. As to whether the net influence on the authority of party leaders is positive or negative, the consensus is firmly the latter.

Additional questions follow in the wake of this discussion. First, is the perceived decline in party leader influence measurable? Second, what are the effects of any such decline on the capacity of the legislature as a whole? Our survey and interview data do not address the question of measurement. Now that term limits have begun to take effect in a number of states, however, roll-call voting data should be available that will make it possible to determine whether levels of voting cohesiveness within parties decline in the post–term limits era relative to the pre–term limits period.

Our survey and interview data suggest that this line of inquiry would be promising. With respect to the second question, our interview subjects suggest that a decrease in the influence of party leaders undermines legislative capacity more generally. According to Senate President Lockyer,

> *Lockyer:* In terms of authority, the one source of tension is between the leaders of each caucus and the committee members, the chairs—what we would call the barons or the dukes and duchesses, and I guess in Congress they call them cardinals. Anyhow, as speakers turn over more readily, that tends to make the central leadership weaker, vis-à-vis, the committee chair.
> *Interviewer:* In the Assembly?
> *Lockyer:* Yes. Now the committee chairs are also weaker because of the lack of experience and expertise vis-à-vis the bureaucracy, the lobbyists, the executive branch and so on.
> *Interviewer:* So, all in all, if there is a shift in power as a result of term limits, is it toward the executive? Lobbyists? Staffers?
> *Lockyer:* Yes. All three of those.

Lockyer's comments sum up the general sense of our interview subjects regarding the effects of term limits on party leadership and direct attention to the broader institutional context within which parties operate. We have already discussed the interview data on the influence of the executive. We turn now to the other actors to which Lockyer referred—staff, lobbyists, and committee chairs.

Effects on Legislative Staff and the Bureaucracy

As with executives, our surveys show that, even controlling for critical characteristics of legislatures such as level of professionalization, legislative staff are perceived to be more influential in term-limit states than in non-term-limit states. Likewise, legislators recognize that staff influence has grown significantly in recent years, since the adoption of term limits. The results with respect to bureaucrats/civil servants are in the same direction, although slightly weaker statistically. That the power of unelected staffers and civil servants grows under term limits is a staple argument among critics of the reform, and most of our interview responses are perfectly consonant with this account, focusing on the destruction of institutional memory and novice legislators' reliance on staff for information about both procedure and policy.

As with party leadership, it is worthwhile to review some of the arguments here, because they illustrate the mechanics by which staff authority might be expected to grow and the specific effects on the policy-making process. According to Speaker Finneran,

> [Staff members] will be the only institutional memory that's available, and it will be inevitable that [their] influence would rise. . . . No matter how honest and bright and hard-working staff may be, legislators themselves have the primary responsibility, and, therefore, I just see this whole area as really enshrining, if you will, legislative staff to the detriment of the legislature as an institution. They are not subject to the same checks and balances and restraints that impose themselves upon us.

The same expectation is voiced in Maine. It is noteworthy, however, that in Maine's far less professionalized and more sparsely staffed legislature, the suspected beneficiary of term limits differs: whereas Finneran focused on staff, Maine House Majority Leader Kontos focuses on civil servants.

> I think where you might see a shift in power is to the nonappointed bureaucrats—I don't like the word *bureaucrats,* but state employees—who routinely come before our committees. These are folks who are not affected by term limits, are in many cases classified appointments, so their position does not rely on whoever is sitting in the governor's office. They are people, in some cases, with twenty or twenty-five years of experience in their departments, and they, then, have a lot of information which should be good for a committee, but they also don't have members of the committee with much of a history on the issues to challenge them, to question them, to demand more information. And I see the shift in power actually moving to some of those folks who routinely work with the legislature, not in a bad way, necessarily, but they won't automatically have the same level of scrutiny at the committee level because you have inexperienced committee members.

The same theme regarding civil servants is echoed in Washington by House Finance Committee Chair Thomas with specific reference to the implications for budgetary oversight and restraint:

> We deal with a lot of bills that are agency requests. We might approve around 15 percent of those sorts of bills now, but I see that going way up in the years to come, just because there won't be anyone around in the legislature that knows any better than the people in the agencies. And I think agencies are holding back bills now, waiting.

There is one idiosyncracy with respect to these accounts and our survey results, given that the interview subjects consistently emphasized relative informational advantages as the source of increased staff and bureaucratic influence. The surveys were conducted in 1995, before term limits had removed any senior legislators from office. Thus, one would expect that any growth in staff and bureaucratic influence based on a lack of expertise and experience among legislators themselves should have been a couple of years off, even in the earliest term-limit states. It is possible that the control variables we employ in our statistical analysis do not account for spurious differences between the influence—and changes in the influence—of staff and civil servants in term-limit states versus non-term-limit states. It strikes us as more likely, however, that the survey responses reflect the effects of term limits on staff and bureaucratic influence that were anticipated even in 1995.

Even when we conducted our interviews early in 1997, the first post–term limits cohort of legislators had only recently been sworn in in two states (Maine and California), and the effects of legislator inexperience on reliance on staff and civil servants were just beginning to be felt. Not surprisingly, then, most of the interview responses look forward. As a result, caution is suggested in evaluating the conclusions on staff and bureaucratic influence drawn from the survey and much of the interview data.

Not all the interview responses were purely speculative, however. One interview subject in Maine, in particular, was uniquely well positioned to evaluate the influence of staff over legislative outcomes. Mayo was a five-term member of the lower chamber who, confronting term limits, took the staff position of House clerk. With experience as both a senior legislator and the highest-ranking staffer in the Maine legislature, his opinion on staff influence during the first postlimit term warrants consideration:

> I think the fact that you don't have people who have long tenure and have learned all the tricks of the trade means you're going to have committee chairs that aren't quite as strong. You're going to have departments and agencies of state government that will be able to be more effective in what they want because the chair has less experience. . . . To be quite frank with you, this position that I hold, in the old days, wouldn't have been participating in some of the meetings that I've had to participate in of late, because we have leadership that don't know the ropes, and I have to step in and tell them what the tradition is. In the past, the first Speaker I served with had been a member of this body since I was five years old. I didn't have to tell him a thing. The second Speaker had service since 1978, continuous. This new Speaker, although she has prior service, really didn't have the

exposure to the position of Speaker that some of her predecessors had, so I've had to step up to the plate here because of that. Now, I like to think that I'm a pretty ethical individual and that I tell the Speaker the right way, but it appears to me very clearly that someone in this position could manipulate the process to their own benefit in a lot of ways.

Later, when asked to comment on the most important effect of term limits, Mayo returned to the same theme:

> *Mayo:* I'm very concerned about [the increase in the power of staff]. I'm mainly concerned about that.
> *Interviewer:* Coming from a person in your position, that's interesting, because it would appear that, if the flow of power toward staff were going to directly benefit anybody, it would be someone like you, in the clerk's position.
> *Mayo:* I'm not concerned about me. It's the other people that have positions of power on the staff within this building that I'm concerned about.

On the opposite side of the legislator-staff relationship from Mayo, Dede Alpert (D-CA) is also well positioned to evaluate the importance of staff as an informational resource. Facing limits after three terms in the lower chamber, Alpert was elected to her first term in the Senate in 1996 and was immediately named chair of the Tax and Revenue Committee. As a counterpoint to Mayo, Alpert is interesting in that she concurs with respect to increasing staff influence but puts an altogether more optimistic spin on the account:

> I think [the influence of staff has increased]. I feel like you have to hope that you have good staff with continuing memory and be aware of this. I know that it happened in my committee on the Senate side that [some staffers] have been with this committee through, I think, the last five chairs. So I feel very, very fortunate because they have seen it all and none of this stuff is brand new to them—where it *is* brand new to me; this is a new issue area for me, so that I need lots of help. It's just going to take time for me to get up to speed. I think that's becoming increasingly difficult, and as I said, it is even more so in our lower house, our Assembly, where the turnover is huge.

The juxtaposed positions of Mayo and Alpert are ironic insofar as Mayo, the staffer, regards the increased reliance on staff expertise with skepticism, whereas Alpert regards it with relief. Nevertheless, these two perspectives are highly relevant for two reasons. First, neither Mayo nor Alpert spoke speculatively but rather from the perspective of the first two states where limits took effect. Second, even within their legislatures, Mayo, as an experienced legislator turned staffer, and Alpert, as a first-term senator serving as chair of a money committee, are positioned to be particularly sensitive to the effects of term limits on the legislator-staff relationship.

We previously urged caution in interpreting the positive survey results and the interview data on the growth of staff and bureaucratic power due to informational advantages. That said, it is worth noting that the positions of all our interview subjects are mutually consistent and are consistent with the survey data. These results are strong enough that they warrant consideration, and they suggest that as term limits take effect their influence on the role of staff should be a fruitful area of research.

Effects on Interest Groups and Lobbyists

As with staff and the bureaucracy, claims about interest-group influence are central to both sides of the term-limits debate. Advocates of the reform claim that the influence of monied interests will be reduced because legislators barred from reelection will be less beholden to campaign donors. Opponents counter that term-limited politicians seeking postlegislative positions will be no less—and perhaps more—responsive to groups that can provide either direct employment or financing for subsequent campaigns and that, whatever legislators' future aspirations, interest-group lobbyists will enjoy the same informational advantages as staff and civil servants over inexperienced legislators under term limits. Our survey asked about the influence of interest groups over legislative outcomes and changes in interest group influence. Unlike staff and the bureaucracy, these two questions generated no substantive or statistically significant difference between term-limit and non-term-limit states. As usual, the interview responses shed light on the rationales behind the survey results, in this instance underscoring the difference between responses on interest groups and staff and civil servants.

When asked whether term limits had any effect on the methods or influence of lobbyists, interview respondents were divided about equally among those who saw no change, those who perceived an increase in influence, and those who perceived a decline.[6] Those who perceived an increase generally cited the same informational asymmetries as with staff and civil servants (Mayo, Pingree, Alpert), and as such, their responses do not require repetition here. The responses of those who expected a decrease in interest-group influence, however, reflect two key differences from the responses in the previous section.

First, with respect to information, lobbyists face a substantially greater challenge than do staffers or civil servants in that they do not occupy positions within the institutions of government on which legislators must rely. Rather, lobbyists must compete with other interests, both institutional and noninstitutional, to attract legislators' attention to information and advice. Building a base of legislative "consumers" of this product is expensive, and efforts to cultivate the trust of legislators over time are necessarily lost under term limits. This situation may raise lobbyists' costs of exercising influence over legislation; it inevitably raises the level of uncertainty about the benefits of such efforts. This position is reflected in the comments of House Majority Leader Kontos:

> I think the lobby has its own reason to be a bit nervous because some of their well-cultivated allies, on certain issues or for certain constituencies, have gone, so they're going to have to work harder to identify those folks that are in those policy areas that are going to be acceptable to them, that are likely to speak on their behalf on bills, and so on. So the lobby is going to have to work harder, I believe, and we're seeing some evidence of that already where special interests are asking to make information briefings not just to the committee of jurisdiction but to the legislature as a whole as a way to educate people on their issues.

Kontos recasts the relationship as one in which information travels two ways—to legislators in the conventional sense but also from legislators in establishing who are the viable targets of lobbying efforts. Accumulating this latter type of information and acting on it require lobbyists to start, effectively, from scratch under term limits.

Second, unlike staff and civil servants, lobbyists' influence does not rest entirely on their ability to impart information strategically to legislators but instead also rests on their ability to channel campaign or job resources about which legislators care. Not surprisingly, most legislators hesitated to discuss explicitly this element of the relationship, but some made implicit references or discussed the exchange relationship with respect to others. Senator Patrick Johnston (D-CA), for example, who is serving his last term, stated, "Once you can't be reelected, you see lobbyists when you want to, not because you have to make the scene," suggesting an increased independence from lobbyists' demands in line with the arguments of term-limits proponents. Others are less sanguine, emphasizing that reliance on interest-group favor continues among those seeking postlegislative employment. Here, the comments of Lockyer, one of Johnston's colleagues in the California Senate, already quoted in chapter 3, warrant partial repetition:

> Some [legislators] are preparing to retire, but not many. Some want to lobby or other things. One of the distressing things you see is when a chair . . . of a powerful committee, a year and a half ahead of departure due to term limits, is meeting with the executives of that industry to try to secure employment for when the term ends.

The bottom line with respect to interest groups and lobbyists is that the interview responses, like the survey responses, were more diverse with respect to levels and changes in influence. The substance of the responses is in line with both sides of the debate over the term-limit reform. The lack of agreement about lobbying, in contrast to the consensus about staff and bureaucratic influence, appears to be driven by the fact that lobbyists do not enjoy institutionally privileged positions as providers of information to legislators and by the fact that the other goods lobbyists and interest groups are in a position to provide may not be sought by all legislators.

Effects on Committees and Chairs

When we asked legislators to evaluate the overall influence of committee chairs over legislative outcomes, the survey turned up no difference at all between term-limit and non-term-limit states. This finding could be a result of the timing of the survey, which took place before limits kicked in, removing senior committee chairs from office. The lack of results, however, might also reflect a survey question aimed that was slightly off the relevant target and that, without follow-up through interviews, may have suggested the misguided conclusion that the status of committee chairs is unaffected by term limits. In fact, the changing status of committee chairs was one of the subjects that most engaged our interview subjects—chairs and nonchairs alike—despite the fact that there was no clear consensus on changes in their influence over legislation relative to other actors. What emerges from these discussions is the now-familiar conclusion that some of the changes wrought by term limits erode the status enjoyed by chairs but that there may be offsetting factors as well.

The most obvious source of decline concerns the experience and seniority of chairs, which, almost by definition, decreases precipitously under limits. At the time of our interviews, the effects were most acutely felt in California and Maine, where limits had recently removed virtually all lower chamber chairs from office. In California, first-term senator Alpert directly attributes her position as chair to term limits:

> [Having term limits] probably means you get a quicker shot at being a chair. I would not have been chair. I'm brand-new to the Senate. I've come from three terms in the Assembly, but as a brand-new member of the Senate in other days, you know, I wouldn't become chair of something like Revenue and Taxation. It's because someone left with term limits who was the chair of this committee. And again, you see, on the Assembly side, where the turnover is very rapid, we have so many new people—people who are basically brand-new are chairing committees. That didn't happen before.

In Maine, where all committees are joint between chambers but are directed by cochairs from each chamber, the effects were similarly dramatic. House Clerk Mayo gave an overview:

> Where the dramatic effect of term limits occurs is in the length of experience of committee chairs and the leadership. Fourteen of the seventeen House chairs of our joint committees have no prior experience as a chair. Many of them are, obviously, in their second and third term in the legislature, so those in their second term have exactly two years of experience.

At the level of the legislative process, the impact is more striking. Verdi Tripp (D-ME), beginning his second legislative term and taking over as House chair of the Tax Committee, described the circumstances under which he assumed the role:

> *Tripp:* What term limits does here—and what we have learned term limits has done in the last year—it moves people that want to go more quickly to the leadership positions, and those that don't want to go generally drift away, or they don't run again. So it forces us after only, in my case, two years of learning about the Tax Committee—about which I've probably learned only a fraction, and now I'm in charge of making sure that ten people from the House understand the process—to work the bills through, make sure they come through in time, hold the public hearings and provide as much knowledge as I can to other people while I'm still learning myself. . . . It's exciting for me, sitting here, knowing that I've only

been in two years and someone has the confidence in you to say "Okay, you're going to be Tax Chair." I know a lot of the people who are other chairs, who are in their second term, too, and it's just that the term limit did push us in that direction. But there are only a few people who will rise above the rest to say, "Okay, two years' experience. I'm willing to take that responsibility."

Interviewer: Do you think that's better than a seniority system?

Tripp: I do. Because what it does is it not only rewards those who feel confident of moving ahead and into leadership roles, but it also is like a merit system. They look at what you've done the first two years, whether or not you are a person who cannot get along with the other side, or whether you [can generate] a consensus to pass legislation.

One's evaluation of Tripp's report hangs on one's confidence that political will and self-confidence are more valuable than the experience seniority brings in making good policy. By Tripp's own account, he was feeling his way along at the outset, constrained by time, public-hearing requirements, the obligation to coordinate the activities of ten other committee members, and his own inexperience in public finance but was buoyed by his willingness to learn and his talent as a consensus-builder. Other members of the Maine legislature, however, assess the trade-offs portrayed by Tripp less favorably. Senate Majority Leader Pingree (D), herself having moved into a party leadership position quickly under term limits, was wary:

I think we're seeing more and more inexperienced people in positions of policy and great decision-making power. We have many more second-term committee chairs right now, which, even for someone who has been here four years, I feel like I'm just beginning to understand some complex policy areas. I just don't think that chairs will have the sort of background and experience that they used to have. . . . There are less and less people that you can turn to and say, "Senator so-and-so knows everything about utilities. Let's give him a call."

Senator Johnston (D-CA) illustrated Pingree's point with specific respect to funding requests for correctional facilities.[7] According to Johnston, the chair of the California Assembly's subcommittee on prisons, with more than twenty years experience on the committee, regularly picked apart executive proposals for prison construction during hearings and legislative markup sessions, successfully blocking spending projects deemed wasteful. With the subcommittee chair termed out in 1996 and a less-experienced successor in place, Johnston estimated that the legislature would appropriate funding for the construction of three new prisons during the assembly that began in January 1997.

A noteworthy alternative interpretation was offered by House Finance Committee chair Thomas (R-WA), who holds that in a context of decreasing overall expertise and informational resources, term limits increase the authority of chairs relative to members because chairs control committee staff members, who are increasingly important as the repository of committee knowledge. Staffers, better qualified than many legislators to assess the viability of legislative proposals and realizing that their relationship with all committee members is of limited duration, feel less compelled to work on behalf of the entire committee membership. Already, in the spring of 1997, Thomas reported,

> A number of times this session, staffers have come to me with bills introduced by junior legislators, who are really not fully competent, to ask me what I think they should do with them. In the past, the staff's reaction would have been to help out the members. Now, they tend to defer more to me. So it allows me to block some bills. Look, the chair controls the staff; the staff has the knowledge; knowledge is king. In that way, I think term limits increase the power of chairs.

Given that the overall level of experience in the legislature inevitably decreases under term limits, the ultimate effect of term limits on the balance of power between committee chairs and members is complex. On the one hand, term limits level the playing field somewhat, guaranteeing that the disparity in experience between chair and committee members cannot exceed the length of the legally allowable term. This decline in relative experience appears implicitly to be at the root of Pingree's and Johnston's conclusion that the relative influence of chairs decreases. Thomas's counterargument is fascinating because, more than the others expressed, it explicitly evaluates the relative influence of chairs versus other actors in the legislative process and presents a counterintuitive position based on institutional incentives. Finally, the interview responses on the changing nature of committee chairmanships illuminate why our original survey questions, focusing on overall levels of influence over legislation, yielded no discernible effect of term limits: legislators concur that term limits matter, but they are diametrically opposed on how and why. Once again, the specific accounts offered in our interviews should be useful in guiding more specific research on the effects of term limits on committee organization and performance.

Effects on Relations between Legislative Chambers

Another insight generated during our interviews that has been largely missing from prior debate over term limits concerns effects on interactions between upper and lower chambers. Two themes were most pronounced, both regarding political career trajectories. First, the general career path from lower to upper chamber will lead to an asymmetry of experience between chambers and thus to an increase in senatorial power relative to lower chambers. Second, the electoral aspirations of members of lower houses, and the reactions to these aspirations in the senates, will undermine cooperation between the chambers.

The first argument mirrors all those reviewed previously about how term limits disrupt the flow of expertise among institutional stations along the legislative process. From Maine, Senate President Lawrence said,

> I think the influence of the Senate will increase under term limits as opposed to the House, simply because there is a learning curve. I've heard a lot of first-time legislators say that they don't really hit their stride until their third year. . . . Currently, out of thirty-five senators, we only have three who have never served in the legislature before—despite the fact that we have I think sixteen or seventeen new members, only three of them have never served in the legislature before.

From California, Senator Alpert said,

> Many Assembly people have come over to the Senate, so that I see power shifting dramatically to this house. The experience is here—as the experienced members came over, the experienced staff came over. The Assembly, out of eighty people, I believe thirty-two people are brand-new, and many of them are needing to serve as chairs of committees, and they don't actually—they just don't know process. They may wind up being wonderful, but they just don't have much lead time to learn. So I see power shifting to the chamber that more people are heading to.

It is possible, of course, that the standard lower-to-upper-chamber career trajectory is itself endogenous to the rules governing legislative reelection and will cease to be the norm in the presence of term limits. Something like this phenomenon was suggested in chapter 3 by those who pointed to alternative postlegislative career paths, including elected offices at the county and municipal levels. Among our survey respondents, however, as chapter 5 will show, lower-house members in term-limited legislatures remain very much interested in running for the upper house of the legislature, but career aspirations leading from senates to lower chambers are rare. Thus, according to House clerk Mayo,

> There's no question in my mind that [the Senate is becoming more powerful]. There is no place for a representative to go that's been termed out other than to run for the state Senate. It's the next logical step. So you're going to have a brain drain, if you will, to that end of the hall. . . . There will be some reverse flow and there has been. . . . I believe you'll see an increased number of senators run for the House, but it won't be the level of House members running for Senate.

In addition to shifting power toward upper chambers, some interview respondents suggested that term limits also undermine cooperation between the chambers because of the aspirations—real or perceived—of lower-house members and the reaction among senators. As Mayo put it, once term limits rule out the prospect of building a political career within a legislative chamber, all political transactions are conducted in light of each legislator's potentially competing ambitions.

> *Mayo:* [There is] a tension between the two bodies that wasn't there, that wasn't as heightened, before. Senators are always looking over their shoulder at who—as few as five, or as many as seven House members, depending on how the districts are drawn—within that district may be running against him. That's always been a phenomenon—senators always wondering who's coming after them from down here [in the House]. That will be heightened, and people who know can look at the list right now and say "Well, obviously, this person wants to stay around the legislature, they live in this Senate district. They're obviously running against this Senator two years from now, so we'll kill all his bills when they come down here," and vice versa.
> *Interviewer:* So you think that will affect cooperation between the two chambers?
> *Mayo:* There's no question, in my mind anyway. No question.

In spite of these potential changes in relative power and cooperation, the fact that seats in state senates are apportioned by population in the same manner as seats in lower houses means that a swing in influence toward state senates should not be expected to have as dramatic an influence on policy as an analogous shift would in the U.S. Congress, for example, where small and rural states are dramatically overrepresented in the Senate. Perhaps for this reason, interview respondents did not predict a specific pattern of policy changes as a result of the shift but rather predicted a change in policy-making style. Even so, the changes in power and cooperation noted by our interviewees, largely unanticipated in discussions of the term-limit reform, might ultimately undermine the improvement in legislative functioning that is desired by term limits' most ardent proponents.

Conclusion

The effects of term limits on the various institutions of state government generated substantial statistical results in our surveys and far more attention among our interview subjects than did our inquiries into changes in the composition of legislatures or the behavior at the individual level. This finding caught us somewhat by surprise. We had expected that anticipatory effects of term limits on who runs for and wins legislative seats or on the behavior of incumbents facing imminent departure would show up quickly after term limits were on the books but that institutional changes would filter more slowly into the system. It may be that our data reflect overestimates by our respondents of changes in the performance and relative powers of institutional actors—that is, perhaps our survey and interview subjects responded with precision to our questions about their individual attributes and behavior but were less judicious in reporting on more abstract institutional changes, and thus our results in this area are less reliable. The consistency between our survey and interview data, however, leads us to believe that our results reflect real changes in state legislative institutions. The interviews support our survey results at every turn. The accounts tend toward consensus on precisely those issues that turn up the strongest statistically in the surveys, and they reflect dissensus on the effects of term limits (but not necessarily no effect) on issues where the statistical results from the surveys are weaker, as summarized in table 4.3.

In short, even if one thinks it likely that legislators might be responding with a bit of hyperbole in evaluating the effects of term limits on institutions, the results are substantial. At a minimum, they suggest the direction that future research might pursue. First, our findings overwhelmingly support the idea that term limits shift influence over legislative outcomes toward the executive branch and away from majority party leaders in the legislature. Second, our results suggest—only slightly less forcefully—that term limits increase the relative influence of legislative staff members, civil servants, and perhaps lobbyists over policy outcomes. Third, our studies show that the nature of committee leadership changes radically in

TABLE 4.3. Summary Effects of Term Limits on Legislative Institutions

Projected Effect on	Detected Effect of Term Limits	Evidence
Governor	increase power, because of informational advantage over inexperienced legislators and power to appoint term-limited legislators to executive posts	1995 survey data and legislator interviews
Legislative party leaders	decrease power because future payoffs and sanctions to rank-and-file legislators become less certain, less relevant	1995 survey data and legislator interviews
Legislative staff	increase power because of informational advantages	1995 survey data and legislator interviews
Bureaucrats/civil servants	increase power because of informational advantages	1995 survey data and legislator interviews
Interest groups, lobbyists	mixed; some increased power because of informational advantages and relevance of post legislative employment; but undermine long-term relationships with specific legislators	1995 survey data and legislator interviews
Committee chairs	mixed; experience and policy expertise decline, but promotion of talent may increase in absence of seniority system	1995 survey data and legislator interviews
Relationship between chambers	increase power of senates relative to lower chambers because of experience, informational advantages; undermine cooperation between chambers because lower-chamber members are (perceived as) gunning for senate seats	1995 survey data and legislator interviews

post–term limits legislatures and generally suggest that committee chairs will be less influential than in assemblies where seniority played a greater role in determining one's location in the committee hierarchy.

The overall trend in these changes is toward a decline in the influence of legislators and a corresponding rise in the influence of others—governors, bureaucrats, lobbyists. The most consistent themes running through discourse about these changes are those of informational asymmetries and declining expertise within legislatures, both on matters of procedure and on the substance of policy. This verdict is echoed in Senator Rosenberg's summation:

> I believe [the presence of term limits] will increase the power of the executive. I believe it will increase the power of lobbyists and people from the outside who are going to be here on a continuous basis, for a period longer than we.

Representative Thomas concurred:

> Look, eighty-three out of ninety-eight members of Washington House were not members six years ago.[8] But the fifteen who were and who will be term-limited out of office after this term are among the most experienced, expert legislators. So, term limits won't increase turnover by much, but they will hurt legislative capacity.

The theme of legislatures debilitated by loss of expertise is augmented by arguments about increased incentives for obstructionism between chambers and those (discussed in chapter 3) about decreased incentives for cooperation among individual legislators. The specific sources of legislative decline, thus, are numerous. The broadest and most important conclusion from our data is that term limits damage the policy-making and policy oversight capacities of legislatures relative to other institutional actors.

CHAPTER 5

Effects on the Broader Electoral Arena

It is now widely recognized that term limits on service in the state legislature can have a significant effect on the larger system of electoral offices. This effect was not necessarily intended by term-limit advocates and has not been widely discussed in the literature. To the extent that term limits are supposed to stimulate citizens to move onto the political scene for a prescribed period (or less if defeated) and then go back to their private lives, one might envisage no effects at all on the larger system of elected and appointed public offices. Yet no one really expects all officeholders to renounce progressive ambitions, and probably few people would desire a system in which officeholders at each level had no experience whatsoever at lower levels.

The question of political careers that span multiple offices, however, has rarely been addressed with any degree of specificity. Term-limit supporters' arguments generally imply that limiting the length of service in any one institution will cure the problem of "career politicians." If reelection to the same office is curtailed, the needed compositional, behavioral, and organizational changes will fall into place. Yet as we noted in chapter 1, a central assumption in most legislative theory is that politicians are ambitious and will seek opportunities for other political office rather than political retirement. If term limits do not mean an end to traditionally ambitious politicians, then we should pay close attention to political career opportunities and trajectories. Prohibiting reelection can be expected to change the way politicians think about their futures, but rather than sending them back home after a few terms, such restrictions will affect the way in which they try to move up or around in the system.

The advance of politicians across offices is less automatic than is reelection to the same office. Although current officeholders seeking election to different offices typically have an advantage compared to nonofficeholders, that advantage is not nearly as great as that of officeholders seeking reelection. Therefore, even the most ardent opponents of political careerism advocate prohibitions on reelection to the same office, rather than on election to all public office, as the appropriate tool to curb the evils of incumbency. Virtually the only place that such multioffice restrictions make sense is within state legislatures themselves, and in fact, states have addressed this matter when enacting term-limit laws. Many term-limit states have lifetime bans on service in a given house after completion of the allotted number of years, thereby preventing an individual from circulating between the two houses of the legislature indefinitely (see table 1.1). In one state, Washington, the limits passed (and then overturned) would not have allowed legislators to serve more than fourteen years out of twenty in the legislature, thus again restricting movement back and forth between houses.

Given the absence of restrictions on movement from one office to another, along with the presumed existence of individuals interested in progressive (or lateral or circular) ambition, it is important to inquire about the consequences of term limits beyond their effects on each individual house of a state legislature. As legislators confront the fact that they must leave office within a prescribed time, with many not wanting to return to their former occupations or positions, their calculations necessarily lead them to think in ways that will have spillover effects on other parts of the political system, including the electoral arena. If legislators want to remain in or close to politics, they will seek other elective office or nonelective positions to which they might be appointed. This strategy was clear in the stories related by our interviewees and, in a few instances, by moves already made, such as that of Joseph Mayo from state legislator to clerk of the House in Maine.

In this chapter, we take up the subject of how term limits in state legislatures will affect political careers—especially potential moves between houses of the state legislature and from the state legislatures to Congress. We will focus on these two moves for a number of reasons. First, these are very common pathways in political careers. In the past thirty years, studies have found that just under half of the members of Congress previously served in their state legislatures.[1] Second, these paths—especially the jump to Congress—are highly significant for national politics, particularly in light of research suggesting that former state legislators behave differently in Congress from those with other backgrounds (Berkman 1993). Third, these trajectories are of special concern to political scientists and other election observers, given their long-standing interest in competitiveness in U.S. state legislative and congressional races. Finally, and fortunately, data on state legislative and U.S. congressional races are far more readily available than are those on election or appointment to alternative offices and positions.

Continuing, Circular, and Progressive Ambition

We begin by returning to a question we addressed in chapter 3. Does the prospect of having to leave office at a prescribed time alter the rate at which legislators seek reelection? If so, has any pattern yet been established for the new positions they seek? In chapter 3, we saw that newcomers in term-limited states did not appear eager to leave the legislature: they were just as likely as newcomers in non-term-limited states to say that they would seek reelection. Among old-timers, however, those in term-limited states were more often ready to quit even before limits legally barred their reelection. Here, we look in more detail at those decisions.

Table 5.1 shows responses from legislators who were eligible for reelection—from both term-limit and non-term-limit states—to the question of whether they plan to run for reelection when their present terms expire. While the vast majority of legislators say they will probably or definitely run for reelection, those in term-limited states are somewhat more likely to say that they will not. The difference is small, which in itself is an important finding. Term-limited legislators obviously do not opt out in large numbers because their time horizons are limited by law. This fact helps explain the absence of immediate change observed in chapter 2 in the

TABLE 5.1.   Percentage of Legislators Intending to Run for Reelection in Non-Term-Limit and Term-Limit States

	Run for Reelection?		
Term-timit state	Definitely/Probably	Probably not/ Definitely not	Total (N)
No	88.7	11.3	100.0 (1,902)
Yes	83.0	16.9	99.9 (969)

Question: Do you plan to run for reelection when your present term expires? (Definitely, probably, probably not, definitely not). This table includes members of both upper and lower houses.

Source: 1995 Survey of State Legislators.

Note: Excluded from the base are a small number of legislators in California and Maine who were ineligible to run for reelection in 1996.

types of individuals entering legislative office. It also suggests that most state legislators—even those in term-limited states—remain interested in sustaining their political careers.

As small as these differences are, the analysis in chapter 3 makes us confident that they cannot be explained away by the attributes of the legislators or their districts. Further analysis is useful, however, in providing greater insight into the legislators' tentative decisions and into the effects of the term-limit reform. Table 5.2 shows the results of a slightly different model from that used previously, breaking down the information on term limits to see more precisely how it affects decisions to leave office while retaining other variables known to affect reelection decisions.[2] It shows, first, a number of effects that are unrelated to term limits: characteristics of the legislators themselves, of the legislatures as institutions, and of the individual districts.

Thus, for example, older legislators are less likely to run for reelection than are younger legislators. This finding holds true when other factors are controlled as in table 5.2, but it is most easily seen in the simple percentages of legislators at various ages who say they will probably not or definitely not run for reelection: age forty or less, 7.0 percent; age forty-one to fifty, 8.4 percent; age fifty-one to sixty, 12.3 percent; age sixty-one to seventy, 22.7 percent, and age seventy-one and older, 25.8 percent. Similarly, the longer legislators have been in office, the more likely they say they are to step down.[3] Although some legislators obviously want to remain in office as long as they possibly can, legislators as a whole appear to tire of their jobs (or of running for their jobs), just as people do in other professions, or they perhaps see better opportunities elsewhere. In any event, there is a general tendency to think of not running the longer one has been in office.

Characteristics of the legislature that affect intentions to run for reelection include the level of professionalization of the legislature and the size of the chamber. The greater the level of professionalization, the more likely legislators are to say they will run for reelection; inspection of tabular data suggests that this is a general effect and not simply a product of the small number of extremely professionalized legislatures. In addition, the larger the chamber, the less likely members are to indicate that they will run again, perhaps because the large size leaves them feeling less satisfied about their individual contribution to the governing process.[4] In any event, the effect of legislative size is relatively small, a difference of one hundred members making only a .08 difference in the response.

One characteristic of individual districts—the size of the population—also appears to influence the intention to run for reelection. The coefficient, which is nearly significant at the usual level, suggests that the

TABLE 5.2.   Intention to Run for Reelection, with Controls for Non-Term-Limit and Term-Limit States and Other Variables

Dependent variable:	Intention to run for reelection	
Scale	Definitely = 1, Probably = 2, Probably not = 3, Definitely not = 4	
Independent variables	b	Standard error
Constant	-318.11**	41.13
State has term limits	.51**	.17
Eligibility (ln [years + 1])	-.27**	.08
Term limits * tenure	.03**	.01
Chamber	-.06	.05
Term limits * chamber	.31**	.07
Age	-.03**	.01
Age squared	.00**	0.00
Tenure in office	.04**	.01
Professionalization	-.53**	.06
Size of chamber	.00**	0.00
District population	.00	0.00
Next election	.16**	.02
$N = 2,731$ Adj. $R^2 = .14$		

Source: 1995 Survey of State Legislators.

Note: For definitions of independent variables, see appendix D. This table includes members of both upper and lower houses.

* $p \leq .05$

** $p < .01$ (two-tailed) (For district population, $p = .08$)

larger the district population, the less likely legislators are to consider seeking reelection. This finding, too, may concern job satisfaction, or it may concern the perceived difficulty of winning: other things being equal, campaigning in a larger district requires more money, time, and effort.

This array of individual, institutional, and constituency factors shows the complex forces that lie behind the decisions of legislators (and presumably of other candidates) to run for office.[5] For present purposes, however, they are a prelude to our concern with the effects of term limits. These are shown in the regression by the coefficients at the top of table 5.2. The coefficients show a significant effect of limits, but it is tempered by the length of time until those limits kick in for the individual in question. They also show that the effects of term limits differ for those with more or less tenure and for members of the lower and upper houses. The direction and size of the effects are readily observed in table 5.3, where tenure, eligibility, and chamber are varied. Only a portion of the cells are filled in because of the strong (negative) correlation between previous tenure and the maximum eligibility.

The negative numbers in the top row show that new legislators in term-limit states are slightly more likely to run for reelection than new legislators in non-term limit-states. As tenure grows, however, legislators become less likely to run again, even if one compares individuals with the same remaining eligibility. Alternatively, if one fixes tenure and compares individuals with ever shorter eligibility, they are less likely to run again. For any given legislator, the effects of tenure and eligibility work in tandem, so that individuals move diagonally down the table (from upper right to lower left), decreasing their likelihood of running again as they have completed more service and simultaneously have fewer potential years to anticipate.[6]

Among upper-house members, the effects of term limits are stronger, so that even those with very little service and a relatively long way to go before being termed out are less likely than their counterparts in non-term-limit states to think about running for reelection. The statistical results do not, of course, indicate just why upper-house members are more sensitive to term limits than are lower-house members, but possible explanations are not hard to come by. More lower-house members are just getting started in politics, and it seems logical that they are more eager to explore their new occupation, including its long-term prospects. It is also likely that they see the prospect of remaining in the legislature for a longer period of time, assuming that they might move to the upper chamber, whereas senators are much less likely to move down. Still another possibility is that upper-house members have more often developed contacts and opportunities that open up interesting careers outside the legislature.

TABLE 5.3. The Effects of Term Limits on the Intention to Run for Reelection

Tenure (years)	Eligibility (number of years until term limited out)						
	0	2	4	6	8	10	12
0	—	—	—	-.02 / .23	-.09 / .16	-.15 / .11	-.19 / .06
2	—	—	.12 / .37	.03 / .28	.04 / .29	-.10 / .16	—
4	—	.31 / .56	.17 / .42	.08 / .33	.01 / .26	—	—
6	.66 / .91	.36 / .61	.22 / .47	.13 / .38	—	—	—
8	.71 / .96	.41 / .66	.27 / .52	—	—	—	—
10	.76 / 1.01	.46 / .71	—	—	—	—	—
12	.81 / 1.06	—	—	—	—	—	—

Source: Derived from table 5.2.

Note: "—" indicates combinations of tenure and eligibility that are impossible under most state term limits. That is, most such limits allow at least three terms (six years) and no more than six terms (12 years).

[a] The top (bottom) number in each cell indicates the effect of term limits on members of the lower (upper) house, based on the results in table 5.2. Higher numbers indicate that legislators are less likely to run for reelection. Equation for top row: .505 - .271 (eligibility) + .025 (tenure). Equation for bottom row: .505 - .271 (eligibility) + .025 (tenure) -.055 + .309.

In any event, the difference is sufficiently great that even first-term state senators in term-limit states are more likely than those in non-term-limit states to think about leaving the legislature.

Finally, the combined effect of the entire set of variables shown in table 5.2 is substantial. Consider, for example, a forty-year-old newcomer to the lower house (ninety-nine members) in a highly professionalized state (.60 on our scale) without term limits and a moderate-sized district (50,000). This individual is expected to be very interested in running for reelection (a 1.55 on the 1–4 scale). A sixty-year-old who is elected to the lower house of a larger (149-member), less professionalized legislature (.20) who is from a larger district (125,000) and who has had four years in office is expected to be more hesitant but still prone to run (1.79). In contrast, individuals who match the first two in demographics and experience but who are in the upper house in a term-limit state (with eight and four years, respectively, left in their quotas) are expected to be vacillating (1.97) or leaning toward quitting (2.47). Term limits thus have a significant effect in discouraging state legislators from running for reelection, but that effect is weak to nonexistent among new lower-house members and stronger among longer-serving members, especially those in the upper house.

Term Limits and Progressive Ambition

The results we have just described show that many legislators in term-limit states are less likely than those in non-term-limit states to entertain the thought of running for reelection. But this finding does not necessarily mean they want to return to their roots. Indeed, in chapter 3 we saw that legislators in term-limit states were just as likely as others to see themselves as career politicians and were equally likely to treat their legislative office as a profession. Determining what these termed out legislators will ultimately do was not possible at the time of our survey, as they themselves did not know. Nevertheless, we can gain considerable insight into two kinds of career moves—from the lower to the upper house of the state legislature and from the upper house to the U.S. Congress—and the rest of this chapter will explore this area. Answers are not as obvious as they might at first appear, especially for congressional moves, where more detailed information is available.

First, apart from the legislature itself and possibly Congress, legislators in term-limit states do not appear headed for one particular postlegislative career. We asked our survey respondents whether, after service in the legislature, they were "likely to run for another office, or otherwise sustain a career in politics." Answers included "statewide office," "local office," "appointive office," and "lobbying/consulting." Legislators in term-limit states were no more likely than those in non-term-limit states to indicate any of those areas as a likely career move. All legislators no doubt overestimate the likelihood that they will run for statewide office; yet 20 percent of those in non-term-limit states versus 18.5 percent of those in term-limit states said that doing so was a possibility. For local office, the percentages were 11 and 12 percent, respectively; for appointive office, 15 and 16 percent; and for lobbying/consulting, 4 percent each.

Each of these nonresults is important in its own way. Statewide offices are one of the few ways in which legislators can move to a higher elective office; one might have expected that such a move would have great appeal to career politicians who cannot continue in the legislature. Local office is important because of suggestions that termed-out legislators might now look to lateral or downward moves to keep their hand in elective politics, as was the case with California's House Speaker, Willie Brown, who left the legislature to become mayor of San Francisco. A different sort of concern applies to appointive offices and the lobbying and consulting industry. Many critics of term limits have expressed concern that legislators would seek out such positions, including some that would involve them directly in legislative business. Despite some isolated cases in which legislators we interviewed perceived colleagues to be pursuing postlegislative employment too arduously, any increase in influence for lobbyists under term limits appears to be driven by their informational advantages relative to inexperienced legislators rather than to legislators' own aspirations to lobbying careers. In the future, as they are confronted with an imminent end to their legislative careers, legislators in term-limit states may seek out these other kinds of positions more frequently. But as of the mid-1990s, the adoption of term limits had not caused legislators immediately to reassess their likely careers and to consider upward, parallel, downward, and outward moves to a greater extent than their colleagues in non-term-limit states.

Running for the Upper House

In contrast to the lack of differences with respect to other elective and non-elective positions, there was a substantial difference between lower-house members in term-limit and non-term-limit states in their expressed intention to run for the upper house. Table 5.4 shows that legislators in term-limit states are half again as likely to intend this move. As with responses about running for statewide office, it is likely that these percentages over-estimate actual future candidacies among all legislators, but the point is that legislators in term-limit states more often think seriously about such a move.[7]

Of course, as with the decision to run for reelection, other factors also enter into legislators' thinking about the future. To see whether the term-limit/non-term-limit difference holds up after controlling for other factors, and to shed more light on considerations about moving up to the senate, we turned to the model used earlier for reelection intentions except, of course, that we evaluate it only for lower-house members (and therefore eliminated variables for chamber). The results, after removing variables that proved not to be significant, are shown in table 5.5.[8]

As in the model for seeking reelection to present office, older legislators less often say they are likely to run for the upper house, while those in professionalized legislatures more often say they are likely to run. Interestingly, longer-serving members are also less likely to say they will try for the upper house. Two processes may explain this result. Older members may be more realistic about their chances of winning election to the upper house and more aware of the difficulties entailed in campaigning in a larger constituency. They may also be more ensconced in their present positions and be less willing to risk losing them, even if it means giving up the chance for a position with more nominal power and prestige. Depending on the institutional distribution of power in the lower chamber, they may have achieved more power as a very senior representative than they could as a relatively junior senator.

The coefficients for the term-limit variables indicate that term limits have a strong effect but that the effect is tempered by the length of time until they kick in for the individual in question. Assessing the magnitude

TABLE 5.4.   Percentage of Lower House Members Intending to Run for Election to the Upper House in Non-Term-Limit and Term-Limit States

Term-limit-state	Run for Upper House?		Total (*N*)
	Yes	No	
No	22.3	77.7	100.0 (1,397)
Yes	34.5	65.5	100.0 (684)

Question: After service in the legislature, do you think you are likely to run for another office or otherwise sustain a career in politics?" (Boxes to check included other state legislative chamber.)

Source: 1995 Survey of State Legislators.

of these effects can be done approximately, as in the case of the reelection measure. However, because the dichotomous answer (likely to run, not likely to run) leads us to use logistic regression rather than OLS, the exact effects of term limits depend on legislators' other characteristics. Therefore, table 5.6 illustrates the results using sets of individuals like those used previously—that is, forty-year-old Republicans in a highly professionalized state and sixty-year-old Republicans in a less-professionalized legislature, with varying lengths of tenure and years of maximum eligibility. For each of these individuals, we calculate the probability of running for the

TABLE 5.5. Intention of Members of the Lower House to Run for Election to the Upper House, Controlling for Non-Term-Limit and Term-Limit States and Other Variables

Dependent variable:	Intend to run for upper house = 1, Do not intend to run = 0.	
	b	Standard error
Constant	.04	.94
State has term limits	2.11**	.46
Eligibility (ln [years + 1])	-.84**	.24
Age	-.01	.04
Age squared	-.00	.00
Tenure in office	-.09**	.02
Professionalization	.61**	.20
Party of legislator	.29**	.11
Independent	.70	.68
$N = 2,050$		
Correctly predicted: 75%		

Source: 1995 Survey of State Legislators.

Note: For definitions of independent variables, see appendix D.

* $p < .05$

** $p < .01$

TABLE 5.6. The Effects of Term Limits on the Likelihood of Lower House Members Running for the Upper House

	40 Year-Old Republican Legislator in a Relatively Professionalized[a] Legislature			60 Year-Old Republican Legislator in a Less-Professionalized[b] Legislature		
	Non-Term-Limit State					
Tenure in office (years)	0	2	4	0	2	4
Probability of running	.50	.46	.42	.21	.18	.16
	Term-Limit State					
Eligibility (ln [years + 1])	9	7	5	9	7	5
Probability of running	.57	.58	.60	.25	.26	.28
Difference in probabilities (states with/without TLs)	.07	.12	.18	.04	.08	.12

Source: Derived from Table 5.5.

Note: We exclude the variable Independent, as it takes on a value of zero in all cases shown. Probabilities of running are determined by multiplying the value of each variable (or the natural logarithm for the eligibility variable) by the coefficient shown for that variable in table 5.5 and summing all the results (plus the constant) to arrive at x and then using the equation $1/(1+e^{-x})$. The value for "eligibility" is the maximum number of years available to a legislator + 1.

[a] .60 on a 0–1 scale. See appendix C.

[b] .20.

upper house in both term-limit and non-term-limit states. The effects of term limits can be seen by comparing the two probabilities, as shown in the bottom row of the table. For those with little past service and a relatively long time available to them, the effect of term limits is relatively small. But the prospect of being termed out makes those nearing the end of their potential service considerably more likely to think that they will run for the upper house, especially when their other attributes make them relatively likely to run even in the absence of term limits.

The types of legislators who are seriously considering running for the upper house in the absence of term limits are the same types that we previously found were interested in running for reelection. They are defined at least by demographics (young), personal experience (relatively little), and a salient institutional characteristic (high professionalization). Term limits add another factor into legislators' calculations about their careers. But the effect of term limits is not simple—all term-limited legislators do not think equally about new careers. Indeed, in their first few years, as noted earlier, legislators in both term-limit and non-term-limit states are not particularly likely to think of moving out. Perhaps such is the case because six to eight years is a long time horizon, especially in the world of electoral politics. Additionally, lower-house members can more readily think about reelection prospects because they can be reelected multiple times (whereas for senators, term limits typically mean that one can only be reelected once), and, if they succeed, they may have the opportunity to remain in the legislature for a considerable length of time by later running for the other chamber. In any event, legislators approaching the designated limits, especially in the upper house, begin to think about not running for reelection (even when they can); for those in the lower house, limited eligibility also stimulates serious thinking about attempting to win election to the other chamber.

Table 5.6 also shows that the effects of time served are different for those in term-limit and non-term-limit states. In non-term-limit states, those with greater tenure are less likely to think about running for the upper house, whereas in term-limit states, those with added tenure are more likely to think about trying for the other house. Tenure per se does not operate differently in the two sets of states: the explanation for this counterintuitive result is that in term-limit states, greater tenure simultaneously reduces legislators' remaining eligibility (and this effect more than offsets the negative impact of tenure as such). As a result, in non-term-limit states, more experienced legislators are likely "to stick around," whereas in term-limit states they are more likely "looking around."

When combined with the insights from our interviews, the differential effects of term limits on the two houses of the state legislature and what these effects might mean for the interaction between the houses are especially intriguing. Senators, it seems, have multiple concerns: in term-limit states they can only remain in office for a fixed time no matter how successful or popular they are; they have to worry about challenges from lower-house members who are being forced out of office;[9] and, unlike lower-house members, they have no upward move in the legislature. Relations between lower- and upper-house members and between the two houses as institutions can hardly be expected to flourish in such an atmosphere, as the interview results reported in chapter 4 suggest. Thus, the individual dynamics that we have uncovered may have spillover effects on the legislature as an institution, helping explain why institutional effects appear so quickly even without obvious changes in the makeup of state legislators.[10]

These results, of course, are based on survey responses about legislators' likely behavior. We do not yet have information on the actual behavior of state legislators that would allow us to judge whether they are in fact trying to move on or up. As we shift our attention to moves from the state legislature to the U.S. Congress, we can observe some of these effects.

Running for Congress

Thus far, we have seen major differences between legislators in term-limit and non-term-limit states with respect to intent to run for reelection and projected movement from state lower houses to senates, but we have detected no difference with respect to running for statewide office and some other political careers. Potential moves from state legislatures to the U.S. Congress initially appear to be more like the latter group than the former. That is, relying on the same survey question about postlegislative career possibilities, legislators in term-limit and non-term-limit states did not differ in their expressed likelihood of running for Congress. Whether we considered all state legislators or only members of the upper house (whom we considered more likely to have given the matter serious thought), the difference was statistically insignificant. Indeed, the relationship, for what it is worth, was opposite that expected—that is, in term-limit states slightly fewer state legislators said they were likely to run for Congress.[11]

In this instance, however, we have information about actual candidacies, making it possible to consider the effects of term limits and other variables on the frequency with which state legislators competed in congressional races. The data on intentions to run are misleading, and there is evidence that term limits were a factor in who ran for Congress even as they were just beginning to go into effect.[12] Because of the power of incumbency, however, ferreting out the effects of term limits is not as straight-forward as it might otherwise be.

Few state legislators ran for the U.S. House in 1994 and 1996 in both term-limit and non-term-limit states.[13] Table 5.7 shows that less than 2.5 percent of all state legislators ran for the U.S. House in each of these two years.[14] Nevertheless, among upper-house members, the 1 percentage point difference between term-limit and non-term-limit states means that almost 50 percent more state senators ran for Congress when faced with term limits.[15] Can this difference between state senators in term-limit and non-term-limit states be attributed to this factor?

Any difference, of course, but especially such a small one, could be explained on the basis of factors that have nothing to do with term limits. Thus, as earlier, we need to develop a model that accounts for those alternative explanations. Among the factors that must be included are whether the congressional seat in question was open or was occupied by an incumbent, whether the incumbent (if there was one) was of the same party as the state senator in question, the partisanship of the district, the number of state senators per congressional district (using the statewide average), whether other state senators (of the same party) are also running,[16] and whether one must give up one's seat to run for Congress.

Modeling congressional candidacies is complicated by the difficulty of gathering the relevant data. A crucial component is determining the congressional district in which state legislators reside. Through a series of steps, we were able to make this determination for more than 80 percent of state legislators serving in the years 1994 and 1996.[17] After discarding an

TABLE 5.7.   Percentage of State Legislators Who Ran for the U.S. House, 1994 and 1996

	Ran for the U.S. House	
Term-limit state	State senators	State representatives
No	2.2 (1,894)	1.1 (5,536)
Yes	3.2 (1,180)	1.2 (2,855)

Source: See note 14.

Note: The base in each cell represents the number of state legislators in that category in 1994 and 1996 combined for whom we could match the district in which the legislator resided.

TABLE 5.8. The Likelihood of a State Senator Running for the U.S. House, Controlling for Term Limits and Other Variables

Dependent variable:	Ran for U.S. House, 1994, 1996 = 1, Did not run = 0			
	b	Standard error	b	Standard error
Constant	-2.65	3.14	-1.91**	.65
State has term limits	3.43**	1.12	2.69**	1.02
Eligibility (ln [years + 1])	2.01**	.59	-1.60**	.54
TL * own party incumbent	.37	.83	.08	.81
TL * other party incumbent	1.72**	.59	1.55**	.58
TL * other state senator(s) in race	.86	.73	1.02[a]	.71
Age	.09[a]	.12	—	—
Age squared	-.00[a]	.00	—	—
Professionalization	-.28	.72	-.40	.69
Own party incumbent running	-3.50**	.51	-3.24**	.47
Other party incumbent running	-2.25**	.43	-2.17**	.42
Other state senator(s) in race	-.91	.57	-.95[a]	.56
District partisanship	.76*	.38	.63	.37
Number of state senators per CD	-.50**	.20	-.52**	.19
Not up for reelection	1.18**	.32	1.03**	.31
Year	.50	.30	.47	.29
	Correctly predicted: 97%		Correctly predicted: 97%	
	N = 2,432		N = 3,025	

Source: 1995 Survey of State Legislators.

Note: For definitions of independent variables, see appendix D.

[a] Age and age squared, and whether any other state senators are in the race, are jointly significant at $p < .05$.

* $p < .05$

** $p < .01$

additional handful of independents on the obvious grounds that they were unlikely to enter a partisan primary, we were left with approximately 3,000 upper-house members for analysis. The results of this analysis appear in table 5.8. In the first model, we include age and age squared because they are important theoretically. But since we do not have age for hundreds of legislators, we include the results without age as well; though the coefficients differ as to specifics, the same set of variables is significant, with roughly similar magnitudes.

As with other decisions about career advancement, the results show the influence of a variety of factors other than term limits. The presence of an incumbent in the relevant House seat, especially if that incumbent is of one's own party, reduces the likelihood of running for Congress. Having a large number of other state senators who might compete for the same seat as well as having another state senator (or senators) actually run, reduces the chances that any given one of them will run. And not having to give up one's seat to run for Congress and having a district with a favorable partisan tilt increase the likelihood that a legislator will try.

Having controlled for all of these factors, term limits still make an important difference to the likelihood that a state senator will run for Congress. As in the case of running for the upper house of the state legislature, we illustrate these effects using various sets of individuals. Here, however, instead of varying age and professionalization, we vary the nature of the competition in the district—that is, whether legislators thinking of running for Congress would have to challenge same-party incumbents, challenge other-party incumbents, or run for open seats. For individuals in each of these situations, we calculate the probability of running for the U.S. House in states both with and without term limits. The results appear in table 5.9.

In the case of the likelihood of running for an open seat, the decisions of other senators are important (see n.16), so we illustrate two cases, one in which no other senators are running and one in which one or more other senators are running. Our examples represent a relatively favorable environment; that is, we assume the state senator is not up for reelection, a competitive partisan district, a moderate number of other state legislators in the district, and the year 1996 (when more state legislators chose to run than in 1994). In this environment, a state senator has a fairly high probability of running if no others are likely to run (.40) and a moderate probability of running for Congress even if others are likely to run (.21).

The second case involves identical circumstances except that the state has term limits (and years of eligibility must be distinguished). As happened with respect to running for reelection, those for whom term limits are well into the future actually may be less likely to run for Congress than

TABLE 5.9. The Effects of Term Limits on the Likelihood of a Prototypical State Senator Running for the U.S. House

Conditions

- senator is young (40 years old) and not up for reelection in the year in question
- state legislature is relatively professionalized (.60)
- congressional district is competitive across parties (partisanship = .50)
- seven state senate seats in the congressional district

Attributes	Open Seat (no other senators running)			Open Seat (other senator(s) running)			Other Party Incumbent Running[a]			Own Party Incumbent Running[a]		
	Non-Term-Limit State											
Probability of running	.40			.21			.07			.02		
	Term-Limit State											
Eligibility (ln [years+1])	5	7	9	5	7	9	5	7	9	5	7	9
Probability of running	.46	.30	.20	.44	.29	.20	.33	.20	.13	.04	.02	.01
Difference in probabilities (states with/without TLs)	.06	-.10	-.20	.23	.08	-.01	.26	.13	.06	.02	.00	-.01

Source: Derived from table 5.8.

Note: Probabilities of running are determined by multiplying the value of each variable (or the natural logarithm for the eligibility variable) by the coefficient shown for that variable in table 5.8 and summing all the results (plus the constant) to arrive at x and then using the equation $1/(1+e^{-x})$. The value for "eligibility" is the maximum number of years available to a legislator + 1.

[a] No other state senators running.

those in non-term-limit states. But as legislators begin to approach the end of eligibility—that is, as term limits begin to become reality—the probability that they will run for Congress increases.[18] The pronounced difference between term-limit and non-term-limit states occurs when other state senators are running. Whereas such competition deters entry into House races for non-term-limited senators, being in a term-limit state essentially means that one ignores whether there is opposition for the party's nomination.

The next case involves seats that are not open—that is, when there is a (congressional) incumbent in the district. In non-term-limit states, the probability of a state senator entering the race is quite low when the incumbent is of the other party (.07) and is extremely low when the incumbent is of the same party (.02).[19] In contrast, in term-limit states, when there is an incumbent of the opposite party, senators are quite likely to run—much more likely than are non-term-limited senators under similar conditions and nearly as likely as under open-seat conditions. Term limits induce fearlessness among state senators in taking on congressional incumbents of the opposite party, particularly as eligibility declines. When there is an incumbent of the same party, conversely, term limits have almost no effect. Even when legislators are faced with imminent departure from the legislature, the norm against taking on an incumbent of one's own party holds.

Term limits thus do not indiscriminately increase the probability that a state senator will opt to run for Congress. They encourage senators to run for open seats, even in the face of stiff competition, and to challenge incumbents of the other party, even early in careers. These effects are more pronounced as future eligibility declines. Thus, term limits, whatever their general effects, interact with opportunity structures, pushing some state legislators along progressive career paths more quickly than might have otherwise occurred and possibly in different ways from those they might have undertaken in the absence of such restrictions.

Competition for Congressional Seats

To this point we have focused on individual legislators and their career paths. But individual decisions have consequences for the system as a whole. Indeed, the point of the term-limit movement is to affect legislatures, not simply to alter the careers of individual legislators. Of the many possible system-level consequences of term limits, we take up here the question of whether term limits will increase competition for congressional seats. Though term limits cannot be applied directly to Congress without a constitutional amendment, their existence at the state level may nevertheless generate a considerable effect. If enough state legislators are persuaded to enter congressional primaries, competition for congressional seats (measured in terms of the proportion of the vote won by challengers) should increase. Moreover, since state legislators (especially senators) are among the most formidable challengers in congressional elections,[20] more congressional incumbents might be persuaded to retire or might be defeated, thus increasing turnover.

The evidence from the previous analysis is suggestive but not definitive. Term-limited state senators are more likely to run for Congress under certain circumstances, sometimes with quite high probabilities. Yet the deterrent power of congressional incumbency on decisions by state senators to run is also evident; we also noted earlier that only a tiny fraction of state legislators run for Congress in any given year. Hence, we need to address the question directly. To do so, we shift our unit of analysis from individual legislators to the congressional primary. Were primaries in 1994 and 1996 more frequently contested by state senators in term-limit states than in non-term-limit states, and can we attribute observed differences to the presence of term limits? We focus on the primary because competition for congressional seats begins there. State legislators who want to run for Congress virtually always begin by contesting a party primary. By concentrating on these contests, we will capture all of the competition that occurs; were we to examine only general elections, we would miss instances in which a senator tried for the nomination and was defeated. The basis for our analysis is therefore the 870 Democratic and Republican primary contests in both 1994 and 1996.[21]

Table 5.10 provides an initial look at the extent of competition in congressional primaries. Just as relatively few state legislators ran for Congress, only a small percentage of congressional primaries are in fact con-

TABLE 5.10.   Percentage of Congressional Primaries Contested by State Legislators in Term-Limit and Non-Term-Limit States

Term-limit state	Congressional Primary Had One or More		
	State senators	State representatives	Senators or representatives
No	4.3	5.6	8.9
Yes	4.5	4.1	7.4

Source: Congressional Quarterly Weekly Report (various issues, 1994, 1996).

tested by one or more state legislators. As earlier, this results, in large part, from the success of incumbents and consequent lack of desire to challenge them. Also in line with earlier results, we find that primaries in term-limit states are very slightly more likely to include state senators but not lower-house members. Notwithstanding the small size of the bivariate difference, it will prove worthwhile to proceed with a multivariate look at whether term limits seem to lead to more frequent competition involving state senators.

Despite the shift in the unit of analysis, many of the same factors are relevant here as in the decisions of individual state senators to run for Congress. Hence, our model of primary competition includes a number of factors that are identical, or nearly so, to those in previous models—incumbency, the level of professionalization of the state legislature, the number of state senators per congressional district, and district partisanship.[22] The term-limit variables are also similar except that in this case the eligibility variable, which can vary across the state senators in a given congressional district, is not included.

The results of this model are shown in table 5.11. As in the prior analyses, the first point to observe is that variables unrelated to term limits play an important role in whether state senators enter a congressional race. If there is an incumbent of either party, but especially of the party holding the primary, it is much less likely that a state senator will run. If the partisanship of the district is favorable to the party holding the primary, it is more likely that a state senator will run. And, finally, if there are, on average, higher numbers of state senators in each congressional district in the state, it is more likely that one or more of them will run. As in table 5.8, the level of professionalization of the state legislature has no significant effect on the likelihood of a state senator being in the race.[23]

As for term limits, their presence alone does not mean that a congressional primary is more likely to include a state senator. Moreover, if an incumbent of the party holding the primary is running for reelection, it is no more likely in term-limit states than in non-term-limit states that the primary has a state senator. But if an incumbent of the other party represents the district, the primary is significantly more likely to have a state senator in the race if there are term limits in that state. These results are more readily interpreted by examining table 5.12.

As shown by the probabilities in the middle of the table, primaries in open-seat districts are relatively frequently contested by state senators, especially in the primary of the party that is favored by the partisan character of the district . Being in a term-limited state does not increase these probabilities. This finding is not surprising inasmuch as open seats present the best opportunity for a state senator or any other potential candidate.

TABLE 5.11.   The Likelihood That a Primary Contest for the U.S. House Includes One or More State Senators

Dependent variable:	One or more state senators ran in a given primary election = 1, No state senators ran = 0.	

	b	Standard error
Constant	-3.07**	.71
State has term limits		
(prior to year of given primary, 1994 or 1996)	.01	.39
Term limits in state * incumbent of this party in race	-.64	.89
Term limits in state * incumbent of other party in race	1.3*	.60
Incumbent of this party in the congressional race	-3.10**	.45
Incumbent of the other party in the congressional race	-2.35**	.42
Professionalization	.13	.70
Number of state senators per congressional district (ln)	.85**	.22
District partisanship	2.04**	.47
Party	-.36	.38
Year (1994)	.29	.38
Party * 1994	-.71	.57
Proportion of state senators up for reelection	-.83	.54
$N = 1,652$		
Correctly predicted: 96%		

Source: Congressional Quarterly Weekly Report and 1995 Survey of State Legislators.

Note: The units of analysis here are the Democratic and Republican congressional primary races in 1994 and 1996. The potential number of cases is thus (435 districts)(two parties)(two years) = 1,740. The N is reduced by the exclusion of districts that were substantially redistricted after 1992. For definitions of independent variables, see appendix D.

 * $p < .05$

 ** $p < .01$

If state senators have any ambition to run for Congress, they are likely to do so when open seats present themselves, regardless of the presence or absence of term limits (except possibly when the legislators have considerable eligibility, according to our earlier results).

In contrast, when an incumbent is running, primaries in general are contested much less frequently (table 5.12, last three columns). But when the primary is in the other party, it is more likely to be contested by a state senator in a term-limited state.[24] Here, then, is where the presence of term limits makes a difference. Challenging an incumbent of one's own party seldom pays off; most such incumbents win, and therefore very few of

TABLE 5.12.   The Effects of Term Limits on the Likelihood That a U.S. House Primary Contest Includes One or More State Senators

Conditions

- relatively professionalized state legislature (.60)
- party primary in 1996
- seven state senate seats in the congressional district
- 50% of state senators in the state are facing reelection

	No incumbent (open seat)			Incumbent of the other party		
District partisanship	.25	.50	.75	.25	.50	.75
	Non-Term-Limit State					
Probability of running	.22	.32	.44	.03	.04	.07
	Term-Limit State					
Probability of running	.22	.32	.44	.09	.14	.21
Difference in probabilities (states with/without TLs)	.00	.00	.00	.06	.10	.14

Note: Probabilities of running are determined by multiplying the value of each variable by the coefficient shown for that variable in table 5.11 and summing all the results (plus the constant) to arrive at x and then using the equation $1/(1+e^{-x})$.

[a]Denotes the probability of a victory for the party in question in an open seat contest in the district in question.

these primaries include a state senator. But given the prospect of being term-limited out, state senators are considerably more willing to enter a primary in which, if they prevail, they will go on to challenge an incumbent of the other party in the general election. The effects are small if measured as absolute differences in probabilities, but when an incumbent runs for reelection, the congressional primary in the other party is three times as likely to include a state senator in term-limit states as in non-term-limit states.

Having found some evidence that term limits stimulate more frequent entry of state senators into congressional primaries, the question arises of whether term limits generate greater competition for congressional seats. This question might be approached in several ways, considering as dependent variables, for example, rates of incumbent retirements and defeats as well as victory margins. As term limits prohibit increasing numbers of state legislators from reelection, we intend to pursue such lines of inquiry. For now, we ask the bottom-line question: Are fewer incumbents returned to Congress from term-limit states than from non-term-limit states? The answer, as of the 1994 and 1996 rounds of congressional elections, is shown in table 5.13 and an associated regression.

Table 5.13 shows the percentage of districts in those two elections in which incumbents were returned to office.[25] The difference between the

TABLE 5.13. Percentage of Incumbents Reelected to Congress in Term-Limit and Non-Term-Limit States

	Incumbent Was Returned to Office		
Term-limit state	Yes	No	*N*
No	81.5	18.5	534
Yes	79.4	20.6	345

Source: Congressional Quarterly Weekly Report and 1995 Survey of State Legislators.

Note: The number of cases is slightly larger than 435 * 2 (years) because of special elections. Members appointed to fill out terms were considered *incumbents* even though they might have been in office only a short time.

percentages is in the direction expected—that is, consistent with the expectation of increased competition from state legislators, a smaller proportion of incumbents is returned in non-term-limit states. Yet the difference is very small, not even close to standard levels of statistical significance. Moreover, in a simple regression model in which we included district partisanship, age, year, and party, the term-limit variable was not significant. Thus, the early evidence suggests that although term limits encourage state senators to run for Congress, the increased numbers are thus far insufficient to displace more than an occasional additional congressional incumbent.

Conclusion

This chapter extends our analysis of the effects of term limits beyond the state legislative chambers in which they are first imposed to the broader electoral environment. At the level of the chambers themselves, we initially find that in term-limit states, even those legislators eligible for reelection are less likely to intend to run than are their brethren in states without restrictions. This effect is driven mainly by long-tenured legislators and by state senators and is absent among legislative newcomers in lower chambers. Term limits thus appear to dampen aspirations for reelection among those with the most experience in the pre–term limits environment.

State legislators, however, are not altogether discouraged about the electoral arena, and their plans reflect slightly accelerated but standard career trajectories of ambitious politicians. That is, lower-chamber members look first to the upper chamber, and state senators look to Congress. Responses to our survey question about intentions to run for the other state legislative chamber show that lower-chamber members in term-limited states are half again as likely as their nonlimited counterparts to aspire to the most proximate office, the state senate. As in earlier chapters, statistical analysis produced a sharper image of the specific factors that encourage this jump. Lower-chamber members in more professionalized states are generally more likely to have an eye on a senate seat. The effect of a legislator's tenure, in contrast, depends on the term-limits status of the state. In the absence of limits, legislators are less likely to plan a run for the senate the greater their tenure, perhaps because in this environment, legislators can expect to enjoy the power and perks of seniority without restriction. In term-limit states, however, tenure is simply the inverse of remaining eligibility for service, so that the expected future benefits of remaining in the lower chamber decline over time. Under these conditions, lower-chamber members are increasingly likely to plan state senate campaigns as their clocks run out.

By the results of our survey alone, term limits would appear to have encouraged "chamber climbing" among professionalized lower-chamber members but to have stranded their senatorial colleagues at the top of the state legislative heap without a clear subsequent career path. Our most straightforward attempt to identify a term-limit effect on progressive ambition—a survey question asking about postlegislative aspirations to Congress, statewide office, and appointed positions—found no difference between term-limited and nonlimited legislators. However, the state senators appeared to be more responsive to term limits in their actions than in their intentions as expressed in the survey. Although only a small percentage ran for Congress, those confronting term limits were more inclined to do so than those not similarly constrained.

Perhaps more interesting, however, was the interaction of term limits with other district-specific conditions in shaping state senatorial decisions to run. As one might expect, a senator's own eligibility in office, the number of other state senators in potential competition for the congressional seat, and the presence of a congressional incumbent all discourage entry into the race. It is remarkable, however, that term limits essentially negate these deterrents when the congressional incumbent is from the opposing party, whereas they have no effect at all when the incumbent is from a state senator's own party. This finding suggests either that the norm of not challenging a congressional incumbent of one's own party has (so far) been impervious to term limits—and the accompanying prospect of political unemployment—or that the parties or incumbents themselves have somehow discouraged intraparty challenges from term-limited senators. Whether this situation remains stable as increasing numbers of state senators must leave office because of term limits warrants close attention. The obverse of this finding is that term limits have encouraged more frequent challenges to congressional incumbents by opposing-party state senators.

From the perspective of the congressional races themselves, as a result, where there is an incumbent, the challenging party's primary is more likely to attract state senators. Whether this situation translates into greater rates of congressional incumbent retirement, defeat, or closer races is still to be determined; the early evidence examined here yields only the hint of a possible increase in congressional turnover.

What do our results in this chapter suggest about the ultimate effect of state legislative term limits on the competitiveness of congressional elections? There are two plausible scenarios. First is that the term-limited state senators prove to be formidable challengers, increasing the competitiveness of congressional elections. If such is the case, then the analysis in this chapter provides specific indications as to when and where we should expect to observe the trickle-up effects of term limits. The other scenario is that, despite an increase in state senatorial candidacies for Congress, competitiveness is unaffected (or declines). Such could be the case if term limits inadvertently lower the quality of these "quality" challengers, forcing state senators out into the arena of congressional campaigns earlier than they would otherwise go—effectively sending the lambs to slaughter at the hands of experienced and non-term-limited congressional incumbents.

Overall, term limits began to create a measurable trickle-up effect on races for some offices even before they began legally to bar large numbers of state legislators from reelection. The anticipation of term limits stimulated substantial numbers of lower-chamber members to plan state senate bids and state senators to enter congressional primaries. Whether the

TABLE 5.14.   Summary Effects of State Legislative Term Limits on the Broader Electoral Arena

Projected Effect on	Detected Effect of Term Limits	Evidence
Intentions to seek reelection (among eligible legislators)	decline, especially among older, more senior legislators and members of upper chambers	1995 survey data
Intentions to run for upper chamber (among lower chamber members)	increase, as eligibility declines, especially among younger legislators in more professionalized states	1995 survey data
Running for Congress	increase willingness of state legislators to run for Congress, even in the face of competition from other state senators or incumbent House members of the opposite party.	U.S. congressional election data, 1994–96
Congressional turnover	slightly higher in term-limit states than non-term-limit states in 1994–1996 (but difference is not statistically significant	U.S. congressional election data, 1994–96

number of aspirant candidates with state legislative experience continues to increase as term limits kick in and whether such an increase has substantial impact on standard measures of competitiveness in state senatorial and/or congressional races will become clear over the course of the next few election cycles.

CHAPTER 6

Taking Stock of Term Limits

"If someone agrees to be a leader he knows how he'll end up. He could hardly expect to die in his bed!" The others laughed. "That'd be a fine thing! Someone rules, commands, then, as if nothing had happened, stops and goes back home." Someone said: "Everybody would want to be a leader then, I'm telling you! Even me, look, I'd be up for it, here I am! . . .

Authority over others is indivisible from the right of those others to have you climb the scaffold and do away with you, one day in the not too distant future. . . . What authority would a leader have without the aura of destiny around him, if you couldn't read it in his eyes, his sense of his end, for every second of his mandate? . . .

Every text setting out the movement's theory reminded the leaders that no exercise of authority was admissible unless by those who had already renounced enjoyment of the privileges of power, those who to all intents and purposes were no longer to be considered as among the living.

Italo Calvino (1923–85), "Beheading the Heads"

In 1969 Cuban-born writer Italo Calvino sketched "a new model for society with a political system based on the ritual execution of the entire governing class at regular intervals" (Calvino 1995).[1] Calvino's ironic account foreshadowed many of the arguments that would surround the debate over legislative term limits in the United States more than two decades later. Fixing in advance a known date of termination sought to attract a different type of politician to office and to alter the nature of the representation provided by those who served, encouraging an elevated detachment from the venality of everyday politics.

Term limits in the United States are less thorough than Calvino's brand. Our politicians, after all, retain their heads. Perhaps as a result, the impact we find on who serves in state legislatures and how they behave does not warrant the label of a "new model for society." Term-limited legislators strongly resemble those who face no guillotine, and they have not renounced the privileges of power. Indeed, they tend to maintain access to political power by seeking reelection when allowed and pursuing progressively higher elected office when the opportunity presents itself or forces itself on them. Within the state legislatures themselves, we find substantial effects of term limits, albeit more mundane effects than those addressed by Calvino. Influence is redistributed away from the traditional power centers of committee chairs and party leaders toward those not subject to term limits, such as executives, civil servants, and staff. In this chapter, we briefly summarize our results and review our main conclusions about the initial effects of term limits on state legislators.

What We Found

This book examines three types of term-limit effects on state legislators and legislatures as well as what could be called trickle-up effects on competition in the broader arena of electoral politics. One of the principal advances we provide is to bring extensive survey, census, and interview data to bear on our questions, allowing us to overcome the most formidable methodological obstacles that have previously hampered research on state legislative term limits. We offer the first direct study of the effects of limits in the U.S. political environment by comparing legislators who are term-limited with those who are not rather than by trying to simulate the condition of term limits by examining some subgroup of legislators, such as those who have announced their retirement, who share some characteristics with term-limited politicians but who should also be expected to differ in important ways.

Composition of Legislatures

We looked first for effects of term limits on the composition of legislatures, and here our results are somewhat surprising. Given that expectations about political career prospects change fundamentally as soon as limits are adopted, one might anticipate the impact of term limits to be felt first in who runs for and wins office. Yet we detect virtually no effect of term limits on the demographics of those elected to state legislatures. There are no systematic differences between term-limit and non-term-limit states in the professional backgrounds, education levels, income levels, age, or ideologies of legislators or in the electoral success of black candidates or religious fundamentalists. The one possible effect relates to the election of women. The states that adopted term limits have tended to elect more women than non-term-limit states both before and after the reforms. Term limits them-selves may have amplified this difference, although in the relatively con-servative electoral environment of the mid-1990s, any effect would have been to mitigate the erosion of electoral prospects for female newcomers rather than to boost their prospects relative to the late 1980s and early 1990s. In any case, the statistical results here are slight enough to warrant cautious interpretation.

Until this study, most analysts of term limits, whether for or against, concurred that the reform would fundamentally alter the composition of state legislatures. Supporters of the reform claimed that term limits would usher a new breed of citizen-legislator into statehouses (Petracca 1991; Will 1992). Among opponents, expectations were summed up most con-cisely by Nelson Polsby, who predicted that term limits would create legis-latures of "the old, the rich, and the bought" (1991:1521). On demo-graphic and ideological grounds, neither side's projections were borne out in the immediate post–term limit electoral cycles. Newcomers in term-limit states displayed the same mix of occupational, educational, ethnic, and socioeconomic backgrounds as their counterparts in non-term-limit states and were equally committed to politics as a vocation. Similarly, we found no evidence that term limits lead to changes in the ideological dispositions of those elected. On liberal-conservative self-placement, newcomers in term-limit states and those in non-term-limit states reflect the same general tendency toward conservatism relative to their predecessors. On specific policy issues, the differences between term-limited and non-term-limited newcomers are either nonexistent or so slight as to be virtually inconse-quential.

Behavior of Legislators

Regarding legislative behavior, we find somewhat more substantial effects, some of which support arguments made by proreform forces and some of which support the case of opponents. Term limits have mixed effects on how legislators budget their time. The legislative leaders we interviewed perceived term limits to encourage legislative individualism and under-mine the cooperation that is sustained by long-term relationships among colleagues. Our surveys found no differences between term-limited and non-term-limited legislators in effort devoted to studying legislation or building coalitions, but our results confirm that newcomers in term-limit states spend more time promoting their own legislation. This much is con-sistent with arguments that reform will stimulate new policy initiatives, although senior legislators tended to criticize the flood of new proposals as either poorly thought out or duplications of ideas that had previously been considered and dismissed. In coming years, it will be worthwhile to determine whether newcomers in term-limit states succeed in shepherding their bills through the legislative process so that the flood of proposals affects the volume of legislation enacted into law. Further, of course, there is the question of whether the substance of law differs in term-limit states and non-term-limit states. On both these counts, it is too early to weigh in with our data, but we can conclude that, for better or worse, new legislators in term-limit states are aggressive policy initiators.

Another behavioral effect of term limits is to decrease legislators' reported effort on some activities for which they are roundly criticized—most notably securing pork for their districts. Consistent with this result, term-limited legislators report placing higher priority than do their non-limited counterparts on the needs of the state as a whole and on the demands of conscience relative to more narrow district interests. Here, as earlier, interpretations of these changes differ according to one's opinion of term limits. Our interview subjects tended to regard reorientation toward statewide issues as exercises in position-taking and legislative showboating, designed to attract media attention and raise the visibility of individual legislators eyeing election to offices with constituencies beyond their current districts. By such an account, strict responsiveness to constituents in the district that is encouraged by unlimited reelection is an important (if suboptimal) means of ensuring political accountability. Most participants in the term-limits debate, however, would likely regard the orientation away from district parochialism as beneficial on the Burkean grounds that term limits encourage legislators to prioritize their perception of the collective good in making policy.

Legislative Institutions

We also searched for effects of term limits at the institutional level and found substantial consequences, both in the survey data and in interviews with senior legislators. The overall effect is best summed up as a redistribution of power within state political institutions away from traditional power centers in the legislatures, particularly committee chairs and party leaders. From the interviews, the principal sources of demise in these legislative institutions are loss of expertise and of the long-term relationships that sustain reciprocal compromise and cooperation. In Maine and California, where the senior legislative cohorts had already been removed by term limits at the time of our interviews, leadership positions traditionally monopolized by longtime members were occupied by relative newcomers who were admittedly dependent on others for policy and procedural expertise. Even in the states where term limits had not yet removed legislators from office at the time of the interviews, Massachusetts and Washington, party leaders and committee chairs noted the decline in their influence over rank-and-file legislators who knew that neither the leaders nor their followers would maintain their positions for long.

These twin forces—decline in expertise and in incentives for cooperation—contribute to influence seeping away from legislatures and toward other policy-making actors, most notably the executive branch and the legislative staff. Although governors in many states have long been subject to term limits, most can draw on richer informational resources, including much larger staffs, than their legislative counterparts. Term limits preclude legislatures from offsetting these executive advantages with the expertise accrued by long-standing party leaders and committee chairs. With regard to legislative staff members, the conventional wisdom suggests that their influence should be greater in the more highly professionalized state legislatures, where personnel are more plentiful and permanent. It may be the case that the increase in staff influence due to term limits is more pronounced where professionalization is greatest. Our interviews, however, suggest that even where legislative resources are scarce, the few repositories of procedural expertise will become increasingly influential and that under term limits these oracles will increasingly be staffers rather than elected officials.

Whereas some term-limit effects on the legislators' behavior at the individual level are consistent with the case made by reform adherents, the institutional effects fall in line with the arguments of detractors. To our knowledge, no term-limit proponents have explicitly listed weakening the political influence of elected lawmakers as a goal of the reforms. Even at this early stage, however, the institutional impact of term limits appears to be in this direction.

Trickle-Up Effects on Electoral Competitiveness

Finally, we sought evidence of term-limit effects outside the legislative chambers to which they directly apply, in the broader arena of electoral politics. We found clear evidence of impact that ripples through the political system, away from the term-limited offices themselves, by pushing incumbent legislators to run for other posts. First, term limits affect legislators' determination to seek reelection, but the effect differs systematically by legislators' status. Freshman legislators in lower chambers are actually slightly more intent on seeking reelection in term-limit states than in non-term-limit states, but as seniority grows, and in state senates generally, term limits increasingly deter legislators from seeking reelection to their current seats, even when they are eligible to do so.

Where do these legislators go? Rather than returning directly to their private stations, many seek other elected office, making the jump as soon as the environment looks promising (or less discouraging), rather than waiting until they are legally removed from their current posts. Term-limited lower-chamber members are more likely to seek state senate seats than are their non-term-limited counterparts, and the effect is most pronounced precisely among those legislators whose prospects for a political career are strongest—younger politicians in states where politics is highly professionalized. Similarly, state senators are more likely to exhibit progressive ambition when confronting term limits. They jump at the opportunity to contest open congressional seats more frequently than if they could remain in the state legislature indefinitely. More strikingly, they are much more likely to challenge incumbent members of Congress from the opposing party than are non-term-limited state senators. As a result, in 1994 and 1996, primary elections for the out party in each congressional district were more likely to include state senators in term-limit states than in non-term-limit states.

These findings suggest that state legislative term limits could increase competitiveness for higher offices—even offices not necessarily subject to limits themselves, such as governorships and other statewide elected offices, as well as state senates—by increasing the pool of candidates for these posts who have prior experience in public office, in fund-raising, and in campaigning. If term limits stimulate the supply of quality candidates who have nothing to lose in running for higher office and are therefore willing to take on incumbents who could otherwise scare off serious challengers, then the rates of incumbent defeats and retirements might be expected to rise. At this point, although we find that a slightly smaller proportion of congressional incumbents was returned to office in term-limit states than in non-term-limit states in the mid-1990s, the difference falls short of conventional levels of statistical significance and so cannot be attributed with any confidence to term limits.

We are confident that the number of "term-limit challengers" for higher office will continue to rise. In this sense there is and will continue to be a trickle-up effect of term limits on the broader system of elections. We are more cautious, however, in predicting a consequent impact on the bottom-line measure of competitiveness, incumbent turnover. It may be that term limits push state legislators toward elections for higher office before these legislators have established the name recognition, campaign organization, and experience to mount successful challenges against incumbents further up the political food chain. Over the next few electoral cycles, as the number of term-limit challengers swells, the seriousness of their threat to incumbents at the higher echelons of elected office will become evident.

Conclusion

In part because the fate of term-limit reforms has been unresolved throughout most of the 1990s, and in part because solid data were lacking, the debate over term limits has been largely polemical. Most analyses have resembled box scores, tallying up arguments and piecemeal evidence as to whether limits are beneficial overall. Inevitably, our study suggests some conclusions along these lines. If the goal is to alter the composition of state legislatures, term limits show no results. If the goal is to discourage district parochialism or to encourage the introduction of bills by junior legislators, the reform shows signs of success. If the goal is to encourage the circulation of elected officials toward higher office, there is evidence of increased willingness by state legislators to challenge for state senate and congressional seats, although there is as yet no strong evidence of increased success. On the downside, there are signs that term limits discourage legislative cooperation, decrease expertise, increase position-taking, and generally weaken legislatures relative to other policy-making actors. It is noteworthy that where we expected to find the biggest effects (in composition), we found little, whereas where we expected to find the smallest effects (on institutions), we found more. In short, for those seeking to size up the early effects of the reform and render a judgment, our evidence suggests a mixed bag of results rather than an open-and-shut case.

With that noted, we see this study as more than just another term limits box score. Limits are the most fundamental electoral reform of the 1990s in the United States. They sever the connection between legislators and voters that is central to how we understand representation through elections. In the absence of this connection, all bets are off as far as drawing on existing theory to explain legislative behavior. One result has been that claims about the effects of term limits staked by political scientists, journalists, politicians, and activists over the past decade have varied wildly, often pointing in opposite directions with respect to the same subject. In the absence of systematic data from the state legislatures themselves, competing claims could not be tested against hard evidence. We attempt to rectify this situation by putting together the first comprehensive, nationwide database on the effects of these reforms, thereby isolating the specific effects of term limits and distinguishing them from other state-specific, district-specific, and time-specific effects that could confound analyses. The effects we find are anticipatory for many states, where limits had not yet kicked in at the time of our research. Yet the results are the more impressive for being preliminary, and we fully expect that the effects we have detected will grow more pronounced over time. Equally as important, our results point to some specific areas—such as district-versus-state-versus-conscience priorities, legislative individualism, decline of policy and procedural expertise, and the effectiveness of term-limit challengers for higher office—that warrant particular attention as we continue to monitor and evaluate the effects of term limits on U.S. politics.

The 1995 State Legislator Surveys

The questionnaires were designed to fit on four 8½-×-11 inch pages (two pages, double-sided). They are shown here in that format but in reduced size.

1. STATE

2. LEGISLATIVE CHAMBER
₁□ Lower House (Assembly)
₂□ Upper House (Senate)
₃□ One Chamber (Nebraska)

3. PARTY
₁□ Democrat
₂□ Republican
₃□ Other

4. INCLUDING THE PRESENT TERM, HOW MANY TERMS HAVE YOU SERVED IN: [CHECK ONE BOX IN **EACH** ROW.]

	0	1	2	3	4	5	6+
Lower Chamber (or Nebraska)	□	□	□	□	□	□	□
Upper Chamber	□	□	□	□	□	□	□

5. WHAT PERCENT OF VOTERS IN YOUR DISTRICT DO YOU THINK FEEL CLOSER TO THE REPUBLICAN PARTY, TO THE DEMOCRATIC PARTY, OR ARE TRULY INDEPENDENT?

_____ %   _____ %   _____ %
Republican   Democrat   Independent

6. WHAT IS YOUR POSITION ON EACH THE FOLLOWING ISSUES?

AGREE STRONGLY	**AGREE SOMEWHAT**	**NEITHER AGREE NOR DISAGREE**	**DISAGREE SOMEWHAT**	**DISAGREE STRONGLY**

It is important to protect a woman's right to legal abortion.
₁□   ₂□   ₃□   ₄□   ₅□

We should have mandatory prayer in the public schools.
₁□   ₂□   ₃□   ₄□   ₅□

We should cut taxes, even if it means deep cuts in government programs.
₁□   ₂□   ₃□   ₄□   ₅□

We should abolish the death penalty.
₁□   ₂□   ₃□   ₄□   ₅□

7. IN GENERAL, DO YOU SUPPORT THE IDEA OF TERM LIMITS FOR

State Legislators: ₁□ Support   ₂□ Oppose   ₃□ No Preference
Members of the U.S. Congress: ₁□ Support   ₂□ Oppose   ₃□ No Preference

8. WHAT DO YOU THINK IS THE RELATIVE INFLUENCE OF THE FOLLOWING ACTORS IN DETERMINING LEGISLATIVE OUTCOMES IN YOUR CHAMBER?   [CHECK ONE BOX IN **EACH** ROW.]

No Influence .... **Dictates Policy**

	1	2	3	4	5	6	7
Majority Party Leadership	□	□	□	□	□	□	□
Minority Party Leadership	□	□	□	□	□	□	□
Committee Chairs	□	□	□	□	□	□	□
Governor	□	□	□	□	□	□	□
Legislative Staff	□	□	□	□	□	□	□
Bureaucrats/Civil Servants	□	□	□	□	□	□	□
Interest Groups	□	□	□	□	□	□	□
Mass Media	□	□	□	□	□	□	□

133

9. IN THE PAST 2-3 YEARS, HAS THE RELATIVE INFLUENCE OF THE FOLLOWING ACTORS CHANGED WITH RESPECT TO DETERMINING LEGISLATIVE OUTCOMES IN YOUR CHAMBER? [CHECK ONE BOX IN **EACH** ROW.]

	Big Decrease 1	Little Decrease 2	No Change 3	Little Increase 4	Big Increase 5
Majority Party Leadership	☐	☐	☐	☐	☐
Minority Party Leadership	☐	☐	☐	☐	☐
Committee Chairs	☐	☐	☐	☐	☐
Governor	☐	☐	☐	☐	☐
Legislative Staff	☐	☐	☐	☐	☐
Bureaucrats/Civil Servants	☐	☐	☐	☐	☐
Interest Groups	☐	☐	☐	☐	☐
Mass Media	☐	☐	☐	☐	☐

10. DO YOU FEEL YOU SHOULD BE PRIMARILY CONCERNED WITH LOOKING AFTER THE NEEDS OF YOUR DISTRICT, OR THE NEEDS OF THE STATE AS A WHOLE?

District   **State as a Whole**

1	2	3	4	5	6	7
☐	☐	☐	☐	☐	☐	☐

11. WHEN THERE IS A CONFLICT BETWEEN WHAT YOU FEEL IS BEST AND WHAT YOU THINK THE PEOPLE IN YOUR DISTRICT WANT, DO YOU THINK YOU SHOULD FOLLOW YOUR OWN CONSCIENCE OR FOLLOW WHAT THE PEOPLE IN YOUR DISTRICT WANT?

Always District   **Always Conscience**

1	2	3	4	5	6	7
☐	☐	☐	☐	☐	☐	☐

12. DO YOU SPECIALIZE IN A SINGLE POLICY AREA OR ARE YOU EQUALLY ACTIVE IN MANY AREAS?

Specialize In   **Equally Active**
Single Policy Area   **In Many Areas**

1	2	3	4	5	6	7
☐	☐	☐	☐	☐	☐	☐

13. IF THIS IS NOT YOUR FIRST TERM, WERE YOU THE PRIMARY AUTHOR OF ANY BILLS OR AMENDMENTS THAT BECAME LAW DURING YOUR LAST TERM?

Bills: $_1$☐ None $_2$☐ One or Two $_3$☐ Three or Four $_4$☐ Five or more
Amendments: $_1$☐ None $_2$☐ One or Two $_3$☐ Three or Four $_4$☐ Five or more

14. HOW MUCH TIME DO YOU ACTUALLY SPEND ON EACH OF THE FOLLOWING ACTIVITIES? [CHECK ONE BOX IN **EACH** ROW.]

	A Great Deal				Hardly Any
Studying proposed legislation	$_1$☐	$_2$☐	$_3$☐	$_4$☐	$_5$☐
Developing new legislation	$_1$☐	$_2$☐	$_3$☐	$_4$☐	$_5$☐
Campaigning/Fundraising	$_1$☐	$_2$☐	$_3$☐	$_4$☐	$_5$☐
Building coalitions within own party to pass legislation	$_1$☐	$_2$☐	$_3$☐	$_4$☐	$_5$☐
Building coalitions across parties to pass legislation	$_1$☐	$_2$☐	$_3$☐	$_4$☐	$_5$☐
Keeping in touch with constituents	$_1$☐	$_2$☐	$_3$☐	$_4$☐	$_5$☐
Helping constituents with problems with government	$_1$☐	$_2$☐	$_3$☐	$_4$☐	$_5$☐
Making sure your district gets fair share of government money and projects	$_1$☐	$_2$☐	$_3$☐	$_4$☐	$_5$☐

15. HOW MANY MILES IS IT FROM YOUR HOME IN THE DISTRICT TO THE CAPITOL?
   ₁☐   ₂☐   ₃☐   ₄☐   ₅☐
   0-30   31-60   61-100   101-150   Over 150

16. WHEN THE LEGISLATURE IS IN SESSION, HOW MANY DAYS PER WEEK, ON AVERAGE, DO YOU SPEND PART OF THE DAY IN THE DISTRICT?
   ☐   ☐   ☐   ☐   ☐   ☐   ☐
   One   Two   Three   Four   Five   Six   Seven

17. WHAT GROUPS DO YOU REGARD AS AMONG YOUR STRONGEST SUPPORTERS? [CHECK **ALL** THAT APPLY.]

☐ Labor/Union   ☐ Business   ☐ Women's Groups   ☐ Christian Coalition
☐ Gun Owner   ☐ Gun Control   ☐ Pro-Life   ☐ Pro-Choice
☐ Farmers   ☐ Pro-Term Limits   ☐ Tax Relief   ☐ Environmentalists

18. DO YOU THINK OF POLITICS AND PUBLIC OFFICE AS A CAREER?   ₁☐ No   ₂☐ Yes   ₃☐ Don't Know

19. IN YOUR MOST RECENT CAMPAIGN FOR THE LEGISLATURE, DID YOU HAVE A CAMPAIGN HEADQUARTERS?
   ₁☐ No   ₂☐ In My   ₃☐ In Friend's   ₄☐ Donated   ₅☐ Rented
               Home   Home   Office Space   Office Space

20. IN THAT CAMPAIGN, DID YOU HAVE A CAMPAIGN MANAGER, COORDINATOR, OR DIRECTOR?
   ₁☐ None   ₂☐ Part-time   ₃☐ Part-time   ₄☐ Full-time   ₅☐ Full-time
               Volunteer   Paid   Volunteer   Paid

21. DID YOU TAKE A POSITION ON TERM LIMITS DURING YOUR LAST CAMPAIGN?
   ₁☐ No Position   ₂☐ Favored   ₃☐ Opposed

22. WERE YOU OPPOSED IN YOUR LAST CAMPAIGN?
   Primary Election   ₁☐ No ₂☐ Yes   **General Election**   ₁☐ No ₂☐ Yes

23. IF OPPOSED IN THAT CAMPAIGN, WHAT PERCENT OF THE VOTE WAS WON BY:
   Primary Election   _____% You   _____% 2nd Place Candidate
   General Election   _____% You   _____% 2nd Place Candidate

24. IF OPPOSED IN THAT CAMPAIGN, APPROXIMATELY HOW MUCH MONEY WAS SPENT IN THE:
   Primary Election $_____ By You $_____ By 2nd Place Candidate
   General Election $_____ By You $_____ By 2nd Place Candidate

25. IF OPPOSED IN THAT CAMPAIGN, WHICH OF THE FOLLOWING DESCRIBE THE **2ND PLACE** CANDIDATE? [CHECK **ALL** THAT APPLY.]

	Incumbent	Had Held Other Public Elected Office	Had Held Appointed Public Office	Had Held Party Office	Had Never Held Public Office
Primary Election	☐	☐	☐	☐	☐
General Election	☐	☐	☐	☐	☐

26. HOW WOULD YOU DESCRIBE YOUR POLITICAL VIEWS AND, IF OPPOSED, THOSE OF THE SECOND PLACE CANDIDATE IN YOUR LAST CAMPAIGN?

	Extremely Liberal 1	Liberal 2	Slightly Liberal 3	Moderate/Middle of the Road 4	Slightly Conservative 5	Conservative 6	Extremely Conservative 7
YOURSELF	☐	☐	☐	☐	☐	☐	☐
Primary Election 2nd Place Candidate	☐	☐	☐	☐	☐	☐	☐
General Election 2nd Place Candidate	☐	☐	☐	☐	☐	☐	☐

27. PRIOR TO ELECTION TO THE LEGISLATURE, WHAT PUBLIC OFFICES DID YOU HOLD? [CHECK **ALL** THAT APPLY.]

	None	Local/County	Judgeship	Statewide Office	Political Party Office
Appointed	☐	☐	☐	☐	☐
Elected	☐	☐	☐	☐	☐

28. DO YOU PLAN TO RUN FOR REELECTION WHEN YOUR PRESENT TERM EXPIRES?

₁☐ Definitely   ₂☐ Probably   ₃☐ Probably Not   ₄☐ Definitely Not

29. AFTER SERVICE IN THE LEGISLATURE, DO YOU THINK YOU ARE LIKELY TO RUN FOR ANOTHER OFFICE, OR OTHERWISE SUSTAIN A CAREER IN POLITICS?   [CHECK **ALL** THAT APPLY.]

☐	☐	☐	☐	☐	☐
U.S. Congress	Statewide Office	Other State Legislative Chamber	Local Office	Appointive Office	Lobbying/ Consulting

30. OCCUPATION OUTSIDE POLITICS? _____   ₁☐ None

31. DO YOU CURRENTLY WORK OUTSIDE POLITICS?   ₁☐ No   ₂☐ Yes

32. DO YOU PLAN TO RETURN TO YOUR OCCUPATION AFTER YOUR SERVICE IN ELECTED OFFICE?

₁☐ Yes   ₂☐ Other Occupation   ₃☐ Retire   ₄☐ Don't Know

33. YEAR OF BIRTH: 19 _____   **34.** GENDER: ₁☐ Female   ₂☐ Male

35. RACE/ETHNICITY: ₁☐ Asian   ₂☐ Black   ₃☐ Hispanic   ₄☐ Native American   ₅☐ Pacific Islander   ₆☐ White

36. HIGHEST LEVEL OF EDUCATION:

₁☐	₂☐	₃☐	₄☐	₅☐
Grades 0-11	High School Diploma	Some College	College Graduate	Graduate School

37. FAMILY INCOME:

₁☐	₂☐	₃☐	₄☐	₅☐	₆☐	₇☐
Below $25,000	$25,000- $49,999	$50,000- $74,999	$75,000- $99,999	$100,000- $249,999	Above $250,000	Prefer Not To Answer

38. RELIGIOUS AFFILIATION:

₁☐	₂☐	₃☐	₄☐	₅☐	₆☐
Roman Catholic	Jewish	Mainline Protestant	Fundamentalist Christian	None	Other (Specify) _____

1. STATE

2. PARTY
₁☐ Democrat
₂☐ Republican
₃☐ Other

3. GENDER
₁☐ Female
₂☐ Male

4. HOW MANY TERMS DID YOU SERVE IN: [CHECK ONE BOX IN **EACH** ROW.]

	0	1	2	3	4	5	6+
Lower Chamber (or Nebraska)	☐	☐	☐	☐	☐	☐	☐
Upper Chamber	☐	☐	☐	☐	☐	☐	☐

5. IN THE DISTRICT YOU SERVED MOST RECENTLY, WHAT PERCENT OF VOTERS DO YOU THINK FELT CLOSER TO THE REPUBLICAN PARTY, TO THE DEMOCRATIC PARTY, OR WERE TRULY INDEPENDENT?

_____% Republican   _____% Democrat   _____% Independent

6. WHAT IS YOUR POSITION ON EACH THE FOLLOWING ISSUES?

AGREE STRONGLY	AGREE SOMEWHAT	NEITHER AGREE NOR DISAGREE	DISAGREE SOMEWHAT	DISAGREE STRONGLY

It is important to protect a woman's right to legal abortion.
₁☐   ₂☐   ₃☐   ₄☐   ₅☐

We should have mandatory prayer in the public schools.
₁☐   ₂☐   ₃☐   ₄☐   ₅☐

We should cut taxes, even if it means deep cuts in government programs.
₁☐   ₂☐   ₃☐   ₄☐   ₅☐

We should abolish the death penalty.
₁☐   ₂☐   ₃☐   ₄☐   ₅☐

7. IN GENERAL, DO YOU SUPPORT THE IDEA OF TERM LIMITS FOR

State Legislators: ₁☐ Support   ₂☐ Oppose   ₃☐ No Preference
Members of the U.S. Congress: ₁☐ Support   ₂☐ Oppose   ₃☐ No Preference

8. IN THE CHAMBER IN WHICH YOU SERVED MOST RECENTLY, WHAT DO YOU THINK IS THE RELATIVE INFLUENCE OF THE FOLLOWING ACTORS IN DETERMINING LEGISLATIVE OUTCOMES? [CHECK ONE BOX IN **EACH** ROW.]

	No Influence						Dictates Policy
	1	2	3	4	5	6	7
Majority Party Leadership	☐	☐	☐	☐	☐	☐	☐
Minority Party Leadership	☐	☐	☐	☐	☐	☐	☐
Committee Chairs	☐	☐	☐	☐	☐	☐	☐
Governor	☐	☐	☐	☐	☐	☐	☐
Legislative Staff	☐	☐	☐	☐	☐	☐	☐
Bureaucrats/Civil Servants	☐	☐	☐	☐	☐	☐	☐
Interest Groups	☐	☐	☐	☐	☐	☐	☐
Mass Media	☐	☐	☐	☐	☐	☐	☐

9. IN THE PAST 2-3 YEARS, DID THE RELATIVE INFLUENCE OF THE FOLLOWING ACTORS CHANGE WITH RESPECT TO DETERMINING LEGISLATIVE OUTCOMES IN YOUR MOST RECENT CHAMBER? [CHECK ONE BOX IN **EACH** ROW.]

	Big Decrease 1	Little Decrease 2	No Change 3	Little Increase 4	Big Increase 5
Majority Party Leadership	☐	☐	☐	☐	☐
Minority Party Leadership	☐	☐	☐	☐	☐
Committee Chairs	☐	☐	☐	☐	☐
Governor	☐	☐	☐	☐	☐
Legislative Staff	☐	☐	☐	☐	☐
Bureaucrats/Civil Servants	☐	☐	☐	☐	☐
Interest Groups	☐	☐	☐	☐	☐
Mass Media	☐	☐	☐	☐	☐

10. AS A STATE LEGISLATOR, DID YOU FEEL YOU SHOULD BE PRIMARILY CONCERNED WITH LOOKING AFTER THE NEEDS OF YOUR DISTRICT, OR THE NEEDS OF THE STATE AS A WHOLE?

District						State as a Whole
1	2	3	4	5	6	7
☐	☐	☐	☐	☐	☐	☐

11. WHEN THERE WAS A CONFLICT BETWEEN WHAT YOU FELT WAS BEST AND WHAT YOU THOUGHT THE PEOPLE IN YOUR DISTRICT WANTED, DID YOU THINK YOU SHOULD FOLLOW YOUR OWN CONSCIENCE OR FOLLOW WHAT THE PEOPLE IN YOUR DISTRICT WANTED?

Always District				Always Conscience		
1	2	3	4	5	6	7
☐	☐	☐	☐	☐	☐	☐

12. DID YOU SPECIALIZE IN A SINGLE POLICY AREA OR WERE YOU EQUALLY ACTIVE IN MANY AREAS?

Specialize In Single Policy Area						Equally Active In Many Areas
1	2	3	4	5	6	7
☐	☐	☐	☐	☐	☐	☐

13. DURING YOUR LAST TERM, WERE YOU THE PRIMARY AUTHOR OF ANY BILLS OR AMENDMENTS THAT BECAME LAW?

Bills: ₁☐ None ₂☐ One or Two ₃☐ Three or Four ₄☐ Five or more
Amendments: ₁☐ None ₂☐ One or Two ₃☐ Three or Four ₄☐ Five or more

14. HOW MUCH TIME DID YOU ACTUALLY SPEND ON EACH OF THE FOLLOWING ACTIVITIES? [CHECK ONE BOX IN **EACH** ROW.]

	A Great Deal				Hardly Any
Studying proposed legislation	₁☐	₂☐	₃☐	₄☐	₅☐
Developing new legislation	₁☐	₂☐	₃☐	₄☐	₅☐
Campaigning/Fundraising	₁☐	₂☐	₃☐	₄☐	₅☐
Building coalitions within own party to pass legislation	₁☐	₂☐	₃☐	₄☐	₅☐
Building coalitions across parties to pass legislation	₁☐	₂☐	₃☐	₄☐	₅☐
Keeping in touch with constituents	₁☐	₂☐	₃☐	₄☐	₅☐
Helping constituents with problems with government	₁☐	₂☐	₃☐	₄☐	₅☐
Making sure your district got its fair share of government money and projects	₁☐	₂☐	₃☐	₄☐	₅☐

15. HOW MANY MILES WAS IT FROM YOUR HOME IN THE DISTRICT TO THE CAPITOL?

  ₁□   ₂□   ₃□   ₄□   ₅□
  0-30   31-60   61-100   101-150   Over 150

16. WHEN THE LEGISLATURE WAS IN SESSION, HOW MANY DAYS PER WEEK, ON AVERAGE, DID YOU SPENT PART OF THE DAY IN THE DISTRICT?

□   □   □   □   □   □   □
One   Two   Three   Four   Five   Six   Seven

17. DO YOU THINK OF POLITICS AND PUBLIC OFFICE AS A CAREER?   ₁□ No   ₂□ Yes   ₃□ Don't Know

18. IN YOUR MOST RECENT CAMPAIGN FOR THE LEGISLATURE, DID YOU HAVE A CAMPAIGN HEADQUARTERS?

  ₁□ No   ₂□ In My   ₃□ In Friend's   ₄□ Donated   ₅□ Rented
          Home   Home   Office Space   Office Space

19. IN THAT CAMPAIGN, DID YOU HAVE A CAMPAIGN MANAGER, COORDINATOR, OR DIRECTOR?

  ₁□ None   ₂□ Part-time   ₃□ Part-time   ₄□ Full-time   ₅□ Full-time
            Volunteer   Paid   Volunteer   Paid

20. WERE YOU OPPOSED IN YOUR MOST RECENT CAMPAIGN FOR THE STATE LEGISLATURE?

Primary Election ₁□ No ₂□ Yes   **General Election** ₁□ No ₂□ Yes

21. IF OPPOSED IN THAT CAMPAIGN, WHAT PERCENT OF THE VOTE WAS WON BY:

Primary Election _____% You   _____% Your Main Opponent
General Election _____% You   _____% Your Main Opponent

22. IF OPPOSED IN THAT CAMPAIGN, APPROXIMATELY HOW MUCH MONEY WAS SPENT IN THE:

Primary Election $_____ By You $_____ By Your Main Opponent

General Election $_____ By You $_____ By Your Main Opponent

23. HOW WOULD YOU DESCRIBE YOUR POLITICAL VIEWS AND, IF OPPOSED, THOSE OF YOUR MAIN OPPONENT IN YOUR LAST CAMPAIGN?

	Extremely Liberal 1	Liberal 2	Slightly Liberal 3	Moderate/Middle of the Road 4	Slightly Conservative 5	Conservative 6	Extremely Conservative 7
YOURSELF	□	□	□	□	□	□	□
Primary Election Main Opponent	□	□	□	□	□	□	□
General Election Main Opponent	□	□	□	□	□	□	□

24. DID YOU TAKE A POSITION ON TERM LIMITS DURING YOUR LAST CAMPAIGN?

  ₁□ No Position   ₂□ Favored   ₃□ Opposed

25. WHAT GROUPS DID YOU REGARD AS AMONG YOUR STRONGEST SUPPORTERS? [CHECK **ALL** THAT APPLY.]

□ Labor/Union	□ Business	□ Women's Groups	□ Christian Coalition
□ Gun Owner	□ Gun Control	□ Pro-Life	□ Pro-Choice
□ Farmers	□ Pro-Term Limits	□ Tax Relief	□ Environmentalists

26. PRIOR TO ELECTION TO THE LEGISLATURE, WHAT PUBLIC OFFICES DID YOU HOLD? [CHECK **ALL** THAT APPLY.]

	None	Local/County	Judgeship	Statewide Office	Political Party Office
Appointed	☐	☐	☐	☐	☐
Elected	☐	☐	☐	☐	☐

27. WHICH OF THE FOLLOWING DESCRIBE THE PERSON WHO NOW HOLDS YOUR SEAT IN THE LEGISLATURE? [CHECK **ALL** THAT APPLY.]

☐	☐	☐	☐	☐
Had Previously Held Other Public Elected Office	Had Previously Held Appointed Public Office	Had Held Party Office	Had Never Held Public Office	Seat Was Eliminated Through Redistricting

28. WHICH OF THE FOLLOWING BEST DESCRIBES YOUR DEPARTURE FROM THE LEGISLATURE?

₁☐	₂☐	₃☐	₄☐	₅☐	₆☐
Ran For Other Office	Defeated In Primary	Defeated In General Election	Chose To Return To Prior Occupation	Chose To Leave Legislature For New Occupation	Retired

29. IF YOU DID **NOT** RUN FOR REELECTION TO YOUR STATE LEGISLATIVE SEAT, WHY NOT? [CHECK **ALL** THAT APPLY.]

☐	☐	☐	☐	☐	☐	☐	☐
Age/ Illness	Too Frustrating	Too Time Consuming	Too Poorly Compensated	Too Difficult To Win Reelection	Prospect of Term Limits	Better Opportunities Elsewhere	Other (Specify)

_____

30. DO YOU THINK YOU ARE LIKELY TO RUN FOR OFFICE AGAIN, OR OTHERWISE SUSTAIN A CAREER IN POLITICS? [CHECK **ALL** THAT APPLY.]

☐	☐	☐	☐	☐	☐	☐
U.S. Congress	Statewide Office	State Lower House	State Upper House	Local Office	Appointive Office	Lobbying/ Consulting

31. WHILE YOU WERE IN THE LEGISLATURE, DID YOU HAVE AN OCCUPATION OUTSIDE POLITICS? IF SO, WHAT? _____ ₁☐ None

32. CURRENT OCCUPATION: _____ **33.** YEAR OF BIRTH: 19_____

34. RACE/ETHNICITY: ₁☐ Asian ₂☐ Black ₃☐ Hispanic ₄☐ Native American ₅☐ Pacific Islander ₆☐ White

35. HIGHEST LEVEL OF EDUCATION:

₁☐	₂☐	₃☐	₄☐	₅☐
Grades 0-11	High School Diploma	Some College	College Graduate	Graduate School

36. FAMILY INCOME:

₁☐	₂☐	₃☐	₄☐	₅☐	₆☐	₇☐
Below $25,000	$25,000-$49,999	$50,000-$74,999	$75,000-$99,999	$100,000-$249,999	Above $250,000	Prefer Not To Answer

37. RELIGIOUS AFFILIATION:

₁☐	₂☐	₃☐	₄☐	₅☐	₆☐
Roman Catholic	Jewish	Mainline Protestant	Fundamentalist Christian	None	Other (Specify)

_____

Legislator Interviews

Questions

Candidates and Recruitment

Under term limits, do you see a different type of individual running for and winning state legislative seats?

Is it easier or harder to get "good candidates" to run?

Have term limits changed the nature or the source of campaign resources available to candidates?

Constituents and Districts

Have term limits had any impact on your relationship with your constituents in any way?

Specifically, have term limits affected the extent to which legislators are focused on the particular needs of their districts?

Committees

Have term limits had an effect on the importance of committees or the ways in which they operate?

Specifically, has the importance to legislators of positions on particular committees or chairmanships changed under term limits?

Has there been any change in the authority of committee chairs or in the way chairs are selected?

(Do you expect there will be once term limits kick in?)

Inevitably, once term limits kick in, the overall level of experience in the legislature will decline, including that of committee chairs. Do you think this change will affect the effectiveness of chairs in guiding bills through the legislature? In the substance of the legislation itself? Do you see any effects along these lines already?

Legislative Output

> Have term limits changed the way legislators go about their work on legislation? For example, some commentators suggest that legislators will be much more devoted to legislative work under term limits because they only have a short time to realize their agendas. Others suggest that once careers are impossible, legislators will not work as hard to gain expertise on complex policy issues. Do you see any evidence for either of these scenarios?
>
> Have term limits had any impact on the nature or the quality of the legislation ultimately produced? For example, some commentators suggest that under term limits, legislatures will be willing to address difficult issues they previously would have avoided. Any evidence for this?

Balance of Powers

> I'm wondering about how term limits might affect the relative power of different branches of the state government and of different members within the legislature.
>
> In your estimation, do term limits affect the power of the governor relative to the legislature? Why?
>
> What about the influence of legislative staffers?
>
> What about the party leaders? Is their influence over rank-and-file members affected at all by term limits? How?

Interest Groups and Lobbyists

> What about the relationship between lobbyists and legislators? Are lobbyists any more or less influential in shaping policy because of term limits?
>
> Have lobbyists changed the way they approach legislators or the sorts of information they supply because of term limits?

Aspirations

> How much more time are you allowed to serve in this chamber under term limits?
>
> Do you plan to serve the full period you are allowed?
>
> Do you have any plans for what you will do after you leave the chamber?

Generally, do you think term limits change the aspirations of legislators in this chamber? How?

[If so,] Do these changes have any effect on how legislators behave? On the way the legislature as a whole operates?

General Opinion

When they were first proposed in your state, did you support or oppose the idea of term limits?

Any change in your opinion of them by now?

Overall, do you think term limits are a good or bad thing for state politics? Why?

Are there any important effects of term limits that we haven't discussed? What?

Interview Subjects

California

Alpert, Dede (D), chair, Senate Tax and Revenue Committee

Anonymous (D), Assembly committee chair who requested not to be named

Johnston, Patrick (D), chair, Senate Appropriations Committee

Lockyer, Bill (D), Senate president

Maine

Amero, Jane (R), Senate minority leader

Donnelly, Jim (R), House minority leader

Goldthwait, Jill (I), chair, Senate Marine Resources Committee

Gwadosky, Dan (D), former Speaker of the House (1994–96)

Jenkins, John (D), chair, Senate Business and Economic Development Committee

Kieffer, Leo (R), Senate assistant minority leader

Kontos, Carol (D), House majority leader

Lawrence, Mark (D), Senate president

Mayo, Joseph (D), House clerk (1992–97) and former (five-term) House member

Pingree, Chelly (D), Senate majority leader

Tripp, Verdi (D), chair, House Taxation Committee

Massachusetts

   Donovan, Carol (D), member of House Local Affairs Committee
   Finneran, Thomas (D), Speaker of the House
   Lees, Brian (R), Senate minority leader
   Norton, Thomas (D), Senate majority leader
   Rosenberg, Stanley (D), chair, Senate Ways and Means Committee

Washington

   Lisk, Barbara (R), House majority leader
   Thomas, Brian (R), chair, House Finance Committee

APPENDIX C

The Construction of the Professionalization Variable

Level of professionalization has been recognized as a major factor in a host of recent studies of state legislatures. At a general level, there seems to be widespread agreement about how to measure it. As stated by Moncrief and Thompson (1992, 199), the factors that make up professionalization "include increases in session length, members' compensation and benefits, and staffing."[1] Unfortunately, this agreement does not extent to the details of how to measure each component. The measure we use is similar to the one developed by Squire (1992b). It includes each of the three components noted previously and has the virtues of being relatively straightforward, being fairly easy to compute, and yielding a single, cardinal (numerical) measure of professionalization. While small differences in the numeric measure should not be taken too seriously, it is advantageous to have a complete ranking of states for use in regression analyses. In addition, having a numeric score avoids having to make cut points between categories, which are bound to be arbitrary, and distinguishes among states more finely than would a set of ordered categories.

Session Length

Session length was interpreted as the number of days in session in a two-year biennium. Two years were chosen because a small number of states meet only every other year, and other states meet uneven amounts in odd- and even-numbered years. Because the bulk of the legislators in our sample were elected in November 1994, we used the most recent preceding biennium (i.e., 1992–93). Using the "duration of session" as listed in Council of State Governments 1994 (148–53), we calculated the number of calendar days each legislature was in session. We used actual days in session because some states regularly exceed the constitutional or statutory limit; we included both regular and special sessions because of the frequent use of the latter (forty-eight special sessions in twenty-seven states during 1992). There are some obvious cases in which this measure is misleading as an indicator of actual days on which the legislature met: a few legislatures, such as Illinois and Ohio, are listed as having been in session for the entire year. Nonetheless, as a relative measure of the time demands placed on legislators, this choice appears reasonable.

Compensation

Salary figures, as of January 1994, were taken from Council of State Governments 1994 (123–25). For one measure, we used base-pay figures only. For states that provide pay on a per diem basis, we multiplied that figure by the number of days in session (up to the legal maximum). We used pay for a two-year period because of a handful of states that pay legislators differently in odd- and even-numbered years.

For a second measure, we calculated per diem living expenses. These figures are admittedly more problematic. First, they reflect to some degree real expenses incurred, so they are not simply salary augmentation. Second, they are difficult to calculate with a high degree of reliability.[2] Nevertheless, using the same source as for salary, we made an effort to calculate these expenses. Per diem figures (vouchered or unvouchered) were multiplied by the number of days in session for the biennium; where two figures were given, we used the average. We did not count other kinds of compensation (e.g., per diem compensation for committee business) and benefits (e.g., medical insurance and retirement plans). These items are very difficult to compare reliably, and in some cases, data are not readily available to determine compensation over a reasonable time period.

Calculations in the late 1970s show that base pay and total compensation are closely related (Council of State Governments 1978, 31). As Squire (1988, 69) notes, "a ranking of states according to [total compensation] is quite similar to one using the base salary measure." Our data concur.

Staffing

Reliable, meaningful estimates of legislative staff are difficult to calculate and are therefore not generally available. Personal staff arrangements vary widely across legislatures, ranging from year-round staff for all representatives to staff for leaders only to session-only, shared staff. Staffing of committees also varies widely. Following Moncrief's (1988) lead, we therefore opted to use total expenditures on legislative administration (found in U.S. Department of Commerce [various years]). As with session length, we used figures for 1992–93. To avoid double-counting of compensation, we subtracted legislative salaries for the biennium from the expenditure figures. An advantage of the expenditure data is that they are available over a long period of time and are likely to be available into the future, and

TABLE C1.   State Legislative Professionalization: Components and Total Scores
(ordered from low to high by professionalization based on salary only)

State	Legislative Expenses	Days in Session	Annual Salary	Total Compensation	Professionalization	
					Salary Only	Total Compensation
WY	$5,126	93	$3,450	$10,500	.00	.00
NM	$20,574	96	$0	$4,500	.00	.01
ND	$9,527	110	$2,160	$6,720	.01	.00
UT	$19,046	94	$3,825	$10,940	.02	.02
SD	$8,591	136	$4,000	$18,200	.03	.04
MT	$16,229	156	$2,567	$12,934	.04	.05
WV	$20,791	153	$6,500	$23,710	.07	.08
NV	$19,123	166	$7,800	$26,556	.08	.09
KY	$41,418	136	$6,000	$22,173	.09	.09
AL	$29,179	240	$1,050	$15,780	.09	.11
KS	$23,212	194	$6,200	$26,562	.09	.11
ID	$7,306	167	$12,000	$38,162	.10	.10
VT	$6,716	245	$7,870	$30,379	.11	.12
GA	$31,606	150	$10,641	$39,732	.11	.13
AR	$28,286	138	$12,500	$36,316	.11	.11
NH	$15,878	338	$100	$200	.12	.10
MS	$20,486	217	$10,000	$37,794	.13	.14
VA	$41,570	118	$18,000	$46,974	.16	.15
RI	$26,186	393	$300	$600	.16	.14
OR	$31,955	211	$13,104	$42,033	.16	.17
ME	$21,562	315	$8,550	$39,150	.17	.19
NE	$20,289	287	$12,000	$38,207	.17	.18
NC	$36,070	240	$13,026	$52,308	.18	.21
IN	$34,357	273	$11,600	$36,625	.19	.18
LA	$45,810	179	$16,800	$47,025	.19	.18
TN	$25,437	242	$16,500	$52,844	.19	.20
CO	$22,409	245	$17,500	$52,640	.19	.20
IA	$27,140	229	$18,100	$45,125	.20	.18
AZ	30,458	283	$15,000	$44,150	.21	.20

SC	$40,011	368	$10,400	$24,344	.23	.20
MD	$35,090	174	$28,000	$73,052	.24	.23
TX	$132,719	171	$7,200	$29,790	.24	.25
MO	$32,243	266	$22,862	$55,034	.25	.22
CT	$50,002	299	$16,760	$33,520	.25	.21
AK	$43,335	254	$24,012	$81,552	.27	.30
DE	$9,598	347	$24,900	$59,800	.27	.24
HI	$38,933	232	$32,000	$88,360	.30	.30
WA	$88,352	176	$25,900	$63,416	.31	.28
MN	$70,601	237	$27,979	$71,421	.33	.30
OK	$31,522	260	$35,000	$79,100	.33	.28
FL	$182,719	201	$22,560	$54,120	.43	.39
MA	$68,913	724	$30,000	$84,710	.58	.55
WI	$72,195	725	$35,070	$124,515	.62	.66
NJ	$87,434	718	$35,000	$70,000	.64	.54
OH	$53,026	720	$42,426	$84,852	.64	.53
IL	$88,284	731	$38,420	$87,013	.67	.59
MI	$140,738	684	$47,723	$95,446	.78	.65
NY	$304,489	303	$57,500	$141,967	.88	.81
PA	$239,925	674	$47,000	$104,740	.91	.80
CA	$300,622	608	$52,500	$166,408	1.00	1.00

Note: Legislative expenses, days in session, and total compensation are for a biennial period. Expenses, session length, and compensation are from 1992-93. Compensation is that for someone beginning June 1994. Thus, they are intended to reflect the values observed by prospective candidates looking forward to the November, 1994 elections.

[a] In thousands of dollars. Biennial salaries have been subtracted from expenses as reported in the source.

they are highly correlated with the National Conference of State Legislators' 1988 independent measure of staff size (Weberg and Bazar 1988).[3]

Overall Measure

The measures of session length, salary, and expenses were combined to create a single measure of professionalization. Since the three components are not measured on the same scale, some standardization was necessary before they could be combined.[4] We standardized by first calculating a standard deviation score for each state for each separate measure. We then created a simple average of the three components—that is, added the standard deviations and divided by three. Finally, we normalized the resulting scores by setting the lowest score equal to zero and the highest equal to one and adjusting all other scores accordingly.[5] The resulting scores are shown in table C1. Because the two measures (using salary only or total compensation) are so highly correlated, only one needed to be used, and we settled on the former.

Having settled on a single measure of professionalization, we sometimes analyze the components separately because they have occasionally been found to have different relationships with other variables of interest (Moncrief 1988, 128; Weber, Tucker, and Brace 1991). Most often, however, differences among the measures are not systematically related to any well-specified theoretical expectations, which combined with an interest in simplicity, suggest maintaining a single measure. Data on the components of professionalization and the resulting professionalization scores for each state are listed in table C1. Correlations among the components appear in table C2.

TABLE C2.   Correlations among the Components of Professionalization

	Days in Session	Salary	Total Compensation
Legislative expenses	.45	.73	.74
Days in session		.68	.63
Salary			.95

APPENDIX D

Independent Variables for Chapter 5

Variable	Definition/coding
State has term limits	0 = no, 1 = yes
Eligibility	Number of years from 1995 until legislator is unable to run for reelection to the current chamber (1 is added because those in non-term-limit states are initially coded 0, and $\ln(1) = 0$).
Chamber	0 = lower, 1 = upper
Age	Age in years
Tenure in office	Numbers of years in office (capped at 7 due to data availability)
Professionalization	range: 0 (least professional) to 1 (most professional); scale defined in appendix C.
Size of chamber	Number of legislators in chamber
District population	In a state with only single-member districts (SMDs), this is the average district size (total population divided by the number of districts). In multimember districts (MMDs), the population is divided by the number of legislators and the result is multiplied by the average number of legislators per district. (Example: Consider a state with 10 SMDs with 10,000 population each and 10 two-person districts with 20,000 each. The state population divided by the number of legislators is 300,000/30 = 10,000. The average number of legislators per district is $[(10 \times 1) + (20 \times 2)]/30 = 1.6667$. Then, the average population per member is $10,000 \times 1.66667 = 16,667$.)
Next election	Year of next election, 1995–2000

150

District partisanship (for a legislator running for Congress)	0 (least favorable) – 1 (most favorable). In table 5.9, this is the probability of electing a candidate of the legislator's party in the general election in an open-seat race. For the derivation of this variable, see Carey, Niemi, and Powell (2000). In table 5.11, this is the probability of electing a candidate of the party holding the primary.
Incumbent in same (other) party	0 = no, 1 = yes
Number of state senators per district	The number of senators in the state divided by the number of congressional districts in the state.
Other state senators	0 = no other state senators of the same party in this race; senator(s) in race 1 = one or more other state senators of the same party in this race.
Not up for reelection	0 = own seat up in this election cycle; 1 = own seat not up in this election cycle.
Proportion of state senators up for reelection	range: 0 to 1, but usually 0, .5 (staggered terms), or 1
Year dummy variables	0 = 1994, 1 = 1996

Notes

Chapter 1

1. *U.S. Term Limits, Inc. v. Thornton* (115 S. Ct. 1842).

2. *Bates v. Jones*, 97-15864 (December 19, 1997). The Supreme Court declined to hear an appeal on March 23, 1998.

3. For a brief description of the litigation in these three states, see Chi and Leatherby 1998. Those authors fail to note that an earlier term-limit initiative in Nebraska (passed in 1992) was also overturned by the Nebraska Supreme Court (in 1994).

4. In addition, according to the advocacy group U.S. Term Limits, there are at least 2,800 U.S. cities, counties, and towns that impose term limits on elected officials. Many of these restrictions have been enacted only recently, but some date back more than a century (Fagre 1995).

5. In the analysis in this book, we include Massachusetts and Washington among the term-limit states because term limits were in force (though under court challenge) at the time of our survey and interviews as well as at the time of the 1996 elections (used in chapter 5). Term limits were overturned in these states in 1997 and 1998, respectively. We do not include Nebraska as a term-limit state because state term limits were overturned there by the courts twice, definitively in February 1996.

6. All of the twenty-one states that initially acted to limit state legislative terms, plus Alaska and North Dakota, passed measures to limit the terms of their congressional delegations.

7. Very quickly, however, changes that affect length of service in the states will spill over onto Congress. Individuals who are interested in political careers but who are forced out of the state legislatures may consider running for Congress. Indeed, even at this early stage, we see some effects on competition for congressional seats, as discussed in chapter 5.

8. The studies cited focus primarily on Costa Rica, Mexico, and Ecuador, respectively. Term limits also went into effect for the first time in the Philippines in 1996.

9. Of course, the anecdotes often come from those who are committed proponents or opponents of the reform, as are the two authors we cite, so they must be interpreted with extreme caution. For a more systematic though still anecdotal treatment, see Capell 1996. Information from California that includes 1996, the

first year in which legislators were prevented from being reelected, also indicates early effects (Petracca 1998).

10. To contain the cost, we selected 77 percent of the members of lower chambers. The number of legislators sampled in each chamber was proportional to the state population, with a minimum of seventy, or the size of the chamber if it was less than seventy. In addition, we sampled all presiding officers and majority and minority leaders.

11. The response rate was 47 percent. Logistic regression analysis indicated that there were significant differences across a set of individual and contextual variables in the probability of responding. The logistic coefficients were as follows: current rather than former legislator, $-.24$; upper rather than lower chamber, $.20$; days in session over two-year period, $-.0008$; district population (in thousands), $-.0019$; male rather than female legislator, $-.36$; South rather than non-South, $-.44$ (all with $p < .01$, two-tailed). In sum, former legislators, members of upper chambers, members in short-session states, members with small population districts, women legislators, and nonsouthern legislators were more likely to respond. The coefficients from the regression were used to estimate the probability that individuals with given characteristics responded to the survey. These probabilities were then multiplied by the initial selection probabilities to form an overall probability of selection/response. Respondents were then weighted by a factor proportional to the inverse of the overall probability. The factor was chosen so that the number of respondents in the weighted data set was the same as that in the unweighted data set.

12. Our measure of professionalization is described below and in appendix C.

13. Some legislators, or prospective legislators, especially those in states that adopted term limits rather late, may have anticipated their passage prior to their adoption. Fortunately, from a research perspective, the term-limit "revolution" occurred rather quickly, so that anticipation of this sort is likely to have been infrequent.

14. There is widespread agreement that professionalization refers to member compensation, session length, and staffing (e.g., Moncrief and Thompson 1992, 199); unfortunately, agreement does not extend to the details of how to measure each component. Our measure, which is similar to that of Squire (1992b), includes each of these three components and has the virtues of being relatively straightforward, being fairly easy to compute, and yielding a single, cardinal (numerical) measure of professionalization. Details and justification for the construction of our measure are provided in appendix C.

Chapter 2

1. An alternative hypothesis is that individuals who now serve just a few terms and are then defeated might go unchallenged under term limits because potential challengers would simply wait them out, thus turning maximum service into "usual" service.

2. We base these figures on our survey respondents both because the surveys

allow us to distinguish old-timers from newcomers and because later results draw on other elements of the survey data. However, we can compare the aggregate percentages of women among survey respondents in term-limit and non-term-limit states with the same percentages in the whole population (Norrander and Wilcox 1998, 105–6). The percentages are very similar—differing by 0.7 percent in non-term-limit states and 0.6 percent in term-limit states—offering further support for the representativeness of the sample.

3. Diamond 1977 noted that women legislators in the 1960s and 1970s tended to come from less-professionalized legislatures. Recent observations suggest that this difference has largely disappeared (Norrander and Wilcox 1998, 113) as women catch up with and even surpass their male counterparts in terms of political resources and level of political ambition (Carey, Niemi, and Powell 1998).

4. Three of the eleven core southern states (27.3 percent) have term limits (Arkansas, Florida, and Louisiana).

5. Between 1993 and 1995, the proportion of women in state legislatures nationwide increased only 0.1 percent after an average biannual increase of 1.6 percent from 1974 to 1991 (Thomas 1998, 7).

6. The most obvious reason that term limits were adopted in some states and not in others has to do with their provision for initiatives and referendums. Term limits have been adopted in every state whose constitution provides a ballot-initiative mechanism for adopting such reforms and in only one state that does not provide such an opportunity (Carey 1996).

7. The increased number of freshmen could result from more open-seat elections, from greater challenger success against incumbents, or from a combination of both factors. The survey evidence of greater likelihood of retirement among OTTLs leads us to believe that the first factor is more prominent. Also, in other work (Carey, Niemi, and Powell 2000), we found no statistical effect of term limits on the probability of incumbent success in general elections during the 1992–94 electoral cycle. This finding strongly suggests that any anticipatory effect of term limits in increasing turnover is driven by retirements among senior legislators.

Chapter 3

1. One common distinction made in the literature is between western states, with strong populist traditions, and eastern states. The cut here is by no means clean, however. TL states include Maine, Massachusetts, Ohio, and Michigan, whereas NTL states include Minnesota, Wisconsin, Kansas, Texas, and Idaho. The one factor that correlates almost perfectly with whether a state has adopted limits is whether the state's constitution allows for direct democracy through citizen initiatives. In every state where initiatives are allowed, term limits have been adopted, whereas they have been adopted in only one state—Louisiana—where ballot initiatives are not allowed. Moreover, opinion polls consistently show that the idea of term limits is supported by substantial majorities of citizens across regions. Thus, although we include a South versus non-South regional distinction as a control in our analysis, we do not see compelling reasons to expect a priori that

the differences between OTs that we ascribe to term limits are driven instead by region.

2. Another factor may simply be that it is easier for individuals to detect non-cooperative behavior in others than in themselves. The relative timing of the survey and the interviews could also contribute to differences in the results. The survey was conducted during the spring of 1995, after term limits were on the books in twenty states, but before they had kicked in anywhere. The interviews were conducted almost two years later, in the first months of 1997, in four states where their effects should have been the most dramatic—Maine and California, where they had already proscribed reelection for the most senior legislators, as well as Washington and Massachusetts, where they were pending in two and four years, respectively.

3. In addition, newcomers in both types of states report spending slightly less time than old-timers on casework (table 3.5), perhaps because lower visibility or lack of staff deters constituent requests. In any event, we think that this discrepancy is likely to be a perennial difference between new and old legislative cohorts.

4. The result stands in contrast to Carey's (1996) conclusion that long-standing term limits in Costa Rica did not eliminate pork. In that environment, political parties created incentives for legislators to provide particularistic goods (budgetary pork and constituent service) within party-defined bailiwicks out of the belief that particularism electorally helps parties. However, in February 1998, in the closing days of its term, a lame-duck Costa Rican assembly passed a law eliminating the long-standing tradition of bailiwick pork in annual budgets (*La Nación* 1998b). Having allocated the pork to their own bailiwicks for their four-year term, these outgoing legislators were effectively acting to deny their replacements the same opportunity (or obligation, depending on the perspective). The change was denounced by the legislators-elect (*La Nación* 1998a), but the new assembly, once seated, did not immediately overturn the law. We might regard this phenomenon as evidence that the imperative to seek pork is indeed weakened by term limits. Of course, the persistence of bailiwick pork for decades in Costa Rica despite term limits mitigates somewhat against this conclusion.

5. The numbers of legislators and constituents per legislator (using 1990 population figures) in the states in which we interviewed are as follows:

	Number of Legislators in Chamber (average district)	
	Upper Chamber	Lower Chamber
Maine	35 (35,084)	151 (8,132)
California	40 (744,001)	80 (372,000)
Massachusetts	40 (150,411)	160 (37,603)
Washington	49 (99,320)	98 (49,660)

Source: Stanley and Niemi 1998, 20–21, 286–87.

6. Alpert is from San Diego rather than from northern California.

Chapter 4

1. Conversely, it is plausible that there are anticipatory institutional effects. For example, the constraints imposed by norms and rules of procedure may prove less binding on legislators, regardless of their cohort, once term limits impose an end point on existing relationships among institutional actors. If so, then the influence of party leaders over their caucuses, for example, may decrease in term-limit states even before any formal rule changes are adopted.

2. Because our survey was conducted in the spring of 1995, freshman legislators in most states had only been sworn into office a month before the first round of surveys was mailed out.

3. Because we report the results of a number of regressions in each table, clarity of presentation mandates that we present only the coefficients of the independent variable of interest for each equation. As noted, however, each regression contained the same controls as in the regressions in chapters 2 and 3.

4. It is difficult to distinguish between these two interpretations. In our survey, none of the eight institutional actors about which legislators were queried were reported to have lost power, and four were reported to have gained power, suggesting that there is an inherent perceptual bias among respondents toward increasing relative power. Such a bias is certainly not present in interviews, however. When respondents were asked to explain their evaluations of relative power and provide examples, they were far more likely to talk about redistributions of influence in terms of one actor's gains and another's losses.

5. The examples most frequently cited in interviews of goods dispensed by party leaders are committee memberships, which are generally assigned to copartisans by the highest-ranking member of each party caucus in each legislative chamber.

6. For reasons noted in chapter 1, we generally do not count interview responses and report frequencies. Here, however, it is noteworthy that the respondents rendered a split decision.

7. Due to a tape-recorder malfunction, Johnston's original interview transcript is incomplete. However, his account is reconstructed from notes written during the conversation.

8. Six years is the length of Washington's lower-house term limit. Thus, Thomas is underscoring that in the vast majority of cases, the term limit should not be expected to affect tenure.

Chapter 5

1. We put the matter in this way because with more than 7,000 state legislators and only 535 members of Congress, only a small proportion of state legislators run for Congress. We will subsequently return to this point. For data from the 1970s, see Schlesinger 1991, 87; mid-1990s figures appear on the Internet at www.ncsl.org/statefed/ FSLSEN97.HTM (as of October 23, 1998).

2. Excluded are the district demographics used in all tables in chapter 3; most

were unrelated to the decision to run for reelection and, as noted there, were of little interest per se. In preliminary analyses, we also included the partisanship of the legislator, but it was not statistically significant.

3. Our measure of longevity is capped at seven years because of data availability. Inspection of cross-tabulations suggests that the coefficient in table 5.2 is not dependent solely on those who are in the top category (and thus might have been in the legislature for a very long time).

4. One might think this effect results from the chamber itself in the sense that senators are more likely to want to run for reelection than are lower-house members. However, if size of chamber is excluded from the regression, chamber remains nonsignificant.

5. One additional variable—the next year in which the legislator would have to run for reelection—was included in the model because we found that legislators became more decisive about running for reelection as the next election neared (that is, the proportion responding "definitely" versus "probably" intending to run declined for each successive, future election). Without this control, the effects of eligibility and of tenure are likely to be biased.

6. Theoretically, individuals who have no remaining eligibility should say, to a person, that they will definitely not run for reelection, and the entries in table 5.3 should indicate so. That such is not the case results, at least in part, from the fact that as of 1995 all legislators (in term-limit states) had not yet accustomed themselves to the idea that term limits would, in fact, affect them. For example, in our interviews in Massachusetts in January 1997, many legislators seemed remarkably unconcerned about being forced out by term limits. As it turned out, the Massachusetts Supreme Court ratified this disregard, overturning the state's term-limits law later that year.

7. In line with the possibility that legislators in term-limit states would begin to think about rotating between houses, the question asking about intentions to run for the other legislative chamber was asked of senators as well as lower-house members. However, of some 735 senators (excluding Nebraska) responding to the item, only twelve (1.5 percent) listed this possibility as likely (six in term-limit states, five in non-term-limit states, with one anonymous respondent whose state is unknown).

8. Age and age squared were retained because there are strong theoretical reasons for their inclusion and because they are jointly significant. Three variables—TL*tenure, size of chamber, and district population—were not significant, but party was. The variable indexing the next election was not needed because the question asked about intentions after service in the legislature and was not subject to a response effect involving time. Inclusion or exclusion of the nonsignificant variables does not materially affect the impact of the term-limit variables.

9. Lower-house members may often wait until senators' terms are up and thereby compete for open seats. But it has been observed that legislators always seem to worry about their seats even if outside observers think such seats are safe. Moreover, there may, in fact, be some added competition for state senate seats. See our results about congressional races.

10. Some of the same dynamics may affect relationships between junior and senior members of a single house, making it harder for them to work together.

11. In term-limit and non-term-limit states, respectively, 19.5 percent versus 21.7 percent of state senators, and 15.8 percent versus 16.9 percent of lower-house members expressed an intention to run for Congress after service in the state legislature.

12. This finding raises the question of whether reported intentions to run for the upper chamber are reliable. While recognizing that such reports are almost certainly overestimates of subsequent behavior, there is good reason to think that they are more likely to predict actual behavior. First, state lower-house members are probably better positioned to know what running for the upper house entails than state senators are to know what running for Congress entails. For another, the ratio of state lower-house members to upper-house members is smaller than the ratio of senators to members of Congress, so there is considerably more opportunity to run for state senates.

13. Twenty-nine current and (recent) former state legislators ran for the U.S. Senate in 1994 and 1996 (thirteen lower-house members and sixteen state senators). Separate analysis of such a small number of candidacies is unlikely to yield reliable results (and combining them with those running for the House may be misleading because of the differences between House and Senate races). Therefore, we limit the remainder of the analysis to state legislators running for the U.S. House. Our numbers are based on a count of state legislators running in primary elections for the U.S. House using listings in the *Congressional Quarterly Weekly Report*.

14. This estimate is based on some 80 percent of all state legislators for whom we had sufficient information to use in the multivariate model described subsequently. Many individuals served in state legislatures in both years and therefore enter the base twice (as they should). If they ran for the U.S. House in each year, they also enter the numerator twice.

15. We cannot account for the absence of a difference between term-limit and non-term-limit states for lower-house members. It may be attributable, in part, to the fact that representatives typically anticipate more elections even though their term limits are equal in numbers of years.

16. Ideally, one would like to know what kind of competition each senator expected to face at the time the decision to run was made. Not having that information, we use as a proxy the number of state senators in each congressional district (except the focal state senator) who ran. Most state senators interested in running for Congress presumably are aware of the likely decisions of other senators, although admittedly, there is a kind of simultaneity problem in that each one's decision may hinge to some extent on what the others decide.

17. States with only one congressional district presented no classification problem. In states with two or more congressional districts, we relied heavily on the coding of zip codes in each congressional district given in Congressional Quarterly 1993. Whenever it was available from our survey or from mailing lists obtained from the National Conference of State Legislatures, we used the zip code of the legislator's home address; if unavailable, we used the zip code of the district office.

Where zip codes were not wholly in a single district, zip codes of the city in which the legislator resided (using the same source for zip code information) sometimes provided the relevant coding. Some remaining ambiguities were resolved by visual inspection of district boundary lines, shown in Barone, Lilley, and DeFranco 1998. A number of districts in Florida, Georgia, Louisiana, North Carolina, and Texas had to be discarded because post-1992 redistricting made it impossible to determine which zip codes fell into which districts. In each of these states, we retained districts that were unaffected by the redistricting. Information on which seats were redistricted came from Congressional Quarterly (1998).

18. The idea that term limits might make state senators with considerable eligibility less likely to run for Congress is somewhat puzzling. What may account for it is an awareness that not only other state senators but a variety of other officeholders not included in our model, perhaps with better electoral prospects, will choose to run and will have an advantage in the contest for the open seat. In an open seat with favorable partisanship there are on average two high-resource candidates (typically officeholders or former officeholders) entered in a primary. Further, as other senior senators leave the chamber, the opportunities for younger senators to gain position and power in the institution increases, making it more advantageous to stay. In any event, we think that the differences in probabilities are noteworthy

19. This portion of the table assumes that no other state senators are running. If they were, the probabilities would be vanishingly small.

20. Powell (1993) estimated the likelihood of winning a congressional election under comparable conditions to be .38 for state senators; .23–.27 for state representatives, city council members, and state officeholders; .15 for all other officeholders; and lower for nonofficeholders.

21. From this base of 1,740 contests, we excluded those in which redistricting of congressional elections made it impossible to estimate district partisanship (see n.17) and, in 1994, Maine and Montana because late redistricting at the state level might have significantly affected election plans. Some additional cases were subsequently deleted because of missing data on the variables entered into the equation.

22. The measure of incumbency is necessarily slightly different. Here, since the unit of analysis is a party primary, it is whether there is an incumbent of that party (or the opposing party) running for reelection in the district, whereas in table 5.8 it is whether the party of the incumbent, if any, matched that of the state senator running for Congress.

23. Variables relating to party and year and the percentage of state legislators up for reelection were also not significant. We have kept them in the equation because of their theoretical importance. In particular, the party and year variables are important to retain because of the Republican minority-party status going into the 1994 elections followed by its majority-party status in 1996.

24. When the incumbent is in the party holding the primary, the likelihood of a state senator running is very small (.03 or less), whether or not a state has term limits (not shown).

25. These percentages are lower than the more familiar incumbency-reelection

rates because they include cases in which a member of Congress retired or resigned (because the likelihood of a strong challenger could be the cause of a retirement or resignation). The only cases that are excluded are those in which a member of Congress died.

Chapter 6

1. We thank James Johnson for directing our attention to Calvino's writings.

Appendix C

1. Other factors occasionally are referred to as components of professionalization. Berkman 1993, for example, includes the amount of control a state exercises over federal grants in addition to salary, session length, and staffing. More often, only one or two of the three factors are used (e.g., Chubb 1988; Francis 1993; Weber, Tucker, and Brace 1991). Nevertheless, there seems to be reasonable unanimity, especially in recent literature, that these three components collectively identify most clearly the concept of professionalization in state legislatures. In addition to the sources already cited, see Moncrief 1988; Council of State Governments 1992, 129; Squire 1992b.

2. In many states, such expenses are unvouchered, and the ratio of actual expenses to money provided may vary widely among legislators; in other instances, the per diem varies depending on distance from the legislator's residence to the capital. In still other states, one must answer roll call to receive the per diem amount. In one state (Arkansas), expenses are reportedly unvouchered for the senate but vouchered for the house.

3. Using figures for total staff in the legislatures as estimated by NCSL (Weberg and Bazar 1988, 9, using the midpoint of the reported interval) and expenditures for the 1992–93 biennium, the correlation was close to 1. We also considered dividing expenditures by the size of the legislature. However, we decided that overall size of the staff—not size per member—was slightly more desirable theoretically. In any event, overall size and size per capita are correlated at .99.

4. Squire (1992b) compared each measure to a similar measure in Congress, thus showing "how closely a state legislature approximates the professional characteristics of the Congress" (71). While a reasonable decision, we think that a comparison using states alone is more straightforward and captures the main area of interest—the variations among the relative professionalization of states, recognizing that none of them is as fully professionalized as Congress.

5. Since the lowest score (for the salary-only measure) was −.94 and the highest was 2.52, we added .94 to the score for each state and then divided each by 3.46.

References

Interviews

Alpert, Dede. Sacramento, CA. February 27, 1997.
Amero, Jane. Augusta, ME. January 8, 1997.
Anonymous California Assembly committee chair. Sacramento, CA.
    March 10, 1997.
Donnelly, Jim. Augusta, ME. January 8, 1997.
Donovan, Carol. Boston, MA. January 6, 1997.
Finneran, Thomas. Boston, MA. January 6, 1997.
Goldthwait, Jill. Augusta, ME. January 8, 1997.
Gwadosky, Dan. Augusta, ME. January 21, 1997.
Jenkins, John. Augusta, ME. January 8, 1997.
Johnston, Patrick. Sacramento, CA. March 10, 1997.
Kieffer, Leo. Augusta, ME. January 8, 1997.
Kontos, Carol. Augusta, ME. January 8, 1997.
Lawrence, Mark. Augusta, ME. January 8, 1997.
Lees, Brian. Boston, MA. January 6, 1997.
Lisk, Barbara. Olympia, WA. April 28, 1997.
Lockyer, Bill. Sacramento, CA. February 28, 1997.
Mayo, Joseph. Augusta, ME. January 8, 1997.
Norton, Thomas. Boston, MA. January 6, 1997.
Pingree, Chelly. Augusta, ME. January 8, 1997.
Rosenberg, Stanley. Boston, MA. January 6, 1997.
Thomas, Brian. Olympia, WA. April 10, 1997.
Tripp, Verdi. Augusta, ME. January 8, 1997.

Other Sources

Ahuja, Sunil, and Michael K. Moore. 1992. "Tenure in the Senate: Implications
    for the Term Limits Debate." Paper presented at the American Political Science
    Association annual meeting, Washington, DC.
Arnold, R. Douglas. 1990. *The Logic of Congressional Action.* New Haven: Yale
    University Press.
Barone, Michael, William Lilley III, and Laurence J. DeFranco. 1998. *State Leg-
    islative Elections: Voting Patterns and Demographics.* Washington, DC: Con-
    gressional Quarterly.

Barro, Robert J. 1973. "The Control of Politicians: An Economic Model." *Public Choice* 14:19–42.

Berkman, Michael B. 1993. "Former State Legislators in the U.S. House of Representatives: Institutional and Policy Mastery." *Legislative Studies Quarterly* 18:77–104.

Brady, David, and Douglas Rivers. 1991. "Term Limits Make Sense." *New York Times,* October 5, 21.

Breaux, David, and Malcolm Jewell. 1992. "Winning Big: The Incumbency Advantage in State Legislative Races." In *Changing Patterns in State Legislative Careers,* ed. Gary F. Moncrief and Joel A. Thompson. Ann Arbor: University of Michigan Press.

Brown, Clifford W., Lynda W. Powell, and Clyde Wilcox. 1995. *Serious Money: Fundraising and Contributing in Presidential Nomination Campaigns.* New York: Cambridge University Press.

Cain, Bruce E., John A. Ferejohn, and Morris P. Fiorina. 1987. *The Personal Vote: Constituency Service and Electoral Independence.* Cambridge: Harvard University Press.

Calvert, Randall L. 1993. "Communication in Institutions: Efficiency in a Repeated Prisoner's Dilemma with Hidden Information." In *Political Economy: Institutions, Competition, and Representation,* ed. William Barnett, Melvin Hinich, and Norman Schofield. New York: Cambridge University Press.

Calvino, Italo. 1995. *Numbers in the Dark and Other Stories.* New York: Vintage Books.

Capell, Elizabeth A. 1996. "The Impact of Term Limits on the California Legislature: An Interest Group Perspective." In *Legislative Term Limits: Public Choice Perspectives,* ed. Bernard Grofman. Boston: Kluwer.

Carey, John M. 1994. "Political Shirking and the Last Term Problem: Evidence for a Party-Administered Pension System." *Public Choice* 81:1–22.

Carey, John M. 1996. *Term Limits and Legislative Representation.* New York: Cambridge University Press.

Carey, John M., Richard G. Niemi, and Lynda W. Powell. 1998. "Are Women State Legislators Different?" In *Women in American State Legislatures,* ed. Clyde Wilcox. New York: Oxford University Press.

Carey, John M., Richard G. Niemi, and Lynda W. Powell. 2000. "Incumbency and the Probability of Reelection in State Legislative Elections." *Journal of Politics,* forthcoming.

Chi, Keon S. 1997. *State Legislative Term Limits and the Changing Nature of the Legislative Branch.* Working paper. Frankfort, KY: Council of State Governments, Center for State Trends and Initiatives.

Chi, Keon S., and Drew Leatherby. 1998. "State Legislative Term Limits." *Solutions: Policy Options for State Decisions* 6 (1): 1–39.

Chubb, John E. 1988. "Institutions, the Economy, and the Dynamics of State Elections." *American Political Science Review* 82:133–54.

Cohen, Linda R., and Matthew L. Spitzer. 1996. "Term Limits and Representation." In *Legislative Term Limits: Public Choice Perspectives,* ed. Bernard Grofman. Boston: Kluwer.

Congressional Quarterly. 1993. *Congressional Districts in the 1990s.* Washington, DC: Congressional Quarterly.

Congressional Quarterly. 1998. *Congressional Quarterly's Politics in America, 1998.* Washington, DC: CQ Press.

Council of State Governments. 1978. *The Book of the States, 1978–79.* Lexington, KY: Council of State Governments.

Council of State Governments. 1992. *The Book of the States, 1992–93.* Lexington, KY: Council of State Governments.

Council of State Governments. 1994. *The Book of the States, 1994–95.* Lexington, KY: Council of State Governments.

Cox, Gary, and Mathew McCubbins. 1993. *The Legislative Leviathan.* Berkeley: University of California Press.

Daniel, Kermit, and John R. Lott Jr. 1997. "Term Limits and Electoral Competitiveness: Evidence from California's State Legislative Races." *Public Choice* 90:165–84.

Darcy, Robert, Susan Welch, and Janet Clark. 1987. *Women, Elections, and Representation.* New York: Longman.

Diamond, Irene. 1977. *Sex Roles in the State House.* New Haven: Yale University Press.

Dick, Andrew R., and John R. Lott Jr. 1996. "Reconciling Voters' Behavior with Legislative Term Limits." In *Legislative Term Limits: Public Choice Perspectives,* ed. Bernard Grofman. Boston: Kluwer.

Dougan, William R., and Michael C. Munger. 1989. "The Rationality of Ideology." *Journal of Law and Economics* 32:119–42.

Ehrenhalt, Alan. 1991. *The United States of Ambition: Politicians, Power, and the Pursuit of Office.* New York: Times Books.

Everson, David H. 1992. "The Impact of Term Limitations on the States: Cutting the Underbrush or Chopping Down the Tall Timber?" In *Limiting Legislative Terms,* ed. Gerald Benjamin and Michael J. Malbin. Washington, DC: Congressional Quarterly Press.

Fagre, Danielle. 1995. "Microcosm of the Movement: Local Term Limits in the United States." Term Limits Outlook Series, vol. 4, no. 2. Washington, DC: U.S. Term Limits.

Fenno, Richard F. 1978. *Home Style: House Members in Their Districts.* Boston: Little, Brown.

Fiorina, Morris. 1989. *Congress: Keystone of the Washington Establishment.* New Haven: Yale University Press.

Fiorina, Morris. 1992. *Divided Government.* New York: Macmillan.

Fiorina, Morris. 1994. "Divided Government in the American States: A Byproduct of Legislative Professionalism?" *American Political Science Review* 88: 304–16.

Fowler, Linda. 1992. "A Comment on Competition and Careers." In *Limiting Legislative Terms,* ed. Gerald Benjamin and Michael J. Malbin. Washington, DC: Congressional Quarterly Press.

Francis, Wayne L. 1993. "House to Senate Career Movement in the U.S. States: The Significance of Selectivity." *Legislative Studies Quarterly* 18:309–20.

Fund, John H. 1992. "Term Limitation: An Idea Whose Time Has Come." In *Limiting Legislative Terms,* ed. Gerald Benjamin and Michael J. Malbin. Washington, DC: Congressional Quarterly Press.

Garand, James. 1991. "Electoral Marginality in State Legislative Elections." *Legislative Studies Quarterly* 16:7–28.

Gilmour, John B., and Paul Rothstein. 1994. "Term Limitation in a Dynamic Model of Partisan Balance." *American Journal of Political Science* 38:770–96.

Glazer, Amihai, and Martin P. Wattenberg. 1996. "How Will Term Limits Affect Legislative Work?" In *Legislative Term Limits: Public Choice Perspectives,* ed. Bernard Grofman. Boston: Kluwer.

Grofman, Bernard, and Neil Sutherland. 1996. "The Effect of Term Limits When Competition Is Endogenized: A Preliminary Model." In *Legislative Term Limits: Public Choice Perspectives,* ed. Bernard Grofman. Boston: Kluwer.

Herrick, Rebekah, Michael K. Moore, and John R. Hibbing. 1994. "Unfastening the Electoral Connection: The Behavior of U.S. Representatives When Reelection Is No Longer a Factor." *Journal of Politics* 56:214–27.

Herrick, Rebekah, and David L. Nixon. 1994. "Is There Life after Congress? Patterns and Determinants of Post-Congressional Careers." Paper presented at the American Political Science Association annual meeting, Washington, DC.

Hibbing, John R. 1991. *Congressional Careers: Contours of Life in the U.S. House of Representatives.* Chapel Hill: University of North Carolina Press.

Holt, Tom. 1996. "The Changing Legislature: Term Limits and the Oregon Experience." U.S. Term Limits Outlook Series, vol. 5, no. 2. Washington, DC: U.S. Term Limits.

Jacobson, Gary C. 1990. "The Effects of Campaign Spending in House Elections: New Evidence for Old Arguments." *American Journal of Political Science* 34:334–62.

Jacobson, Gary C., and Samuel Kernell. 1981. *Strategy and Choice in Congressional Elections.* New Haven: Yale University Press.

Krehbiel, Keith. 1992. *Information and Legislative Organization.* Ann Arbor: University of Michigan Press.

Lilley, William, III, Laurence J. DeFranco, and William M. Diefenderfer III. 1994. *State Data Atlas: Almanac of State Legislatures.* Washington, DC: Congressional Quarterly Press.

Lilley, William, III, Laurence J. DeFranco, and William M. Diefenderfer III. 1996. *The State Atlas of Political and Cultural Diversity.* Washington, DC: Congressional Quarterly Press.

Lott, J. R., Jr. 1990. "Attendance Rates, Political Shirking, and the Effect of Post-Elective Office Employment." *Economic Inquiry* 28:133–50.

Lott, J. R., Jr., and W. Robert Reed. 1989. "Shirking and Sorting in a Political Market with Finite-Lived Politicians." *Public Choice* 61:75–96.

Malbin, Michael J., and Gerald Benjamin. 1992. "Legislatures after Term Limits." In *Limiting Legislative Terms,* ed. Gerald Benjamin and Michael J. Malbin. Washington, DC: Congressional Quarterly Press.

Matthews, Donald R. 1960. *U.S. Senators and Their World.* New York: Random House.

Mayhew, David R. 1974. *Congress: The Electoral Connection.* New Haven: Yale University Press.

McArthur, J. 1990. "Congressional Attendance and Political Shirking in Lame Duck Sessions." Unpublished paper, May.

Mejía Acosta, Andrés. 1996. "La No-reelección Legislativa en Ecuador." In *Este País: Tendencias y Opiniones.* Mexico City: Desarrollo de Opinión Pública.

Mitchell, Cleta Deatherage. 1991. "Limit Terms? Yes!" In *Extensions.* Norman, OK: Carl Albert Research Center.

Moncrief, Gary F. 1988. "Dimensions of the Concept of Professionalism in State Legislatures: A Research Note." *State and Local Governmental Review* 20:128–32.

Moncrief, Gary F., and Joel A. Thompson, eds. 1992. *Changing Patterns in State Legislative Careers.* Ann Arbor: University of Michigan Press.

Moncrief, Gary F., Joel A. Thompson, Michael Haddon, and Robert Hoyer. 1992. "For Whom the Bell Tolls: Term Limits and State Legislatures." *Legislative Studies Quarterly* 17:37–47.

La Nación. 1998a. "Gobierno regulará partidas." La Nación Digital (www.nacion.co.cr). San José, Costa Rica. February 13.

La Nación. 1998b. "Plan aprobado en primer debate." La Nación Digital (www.nacion.co.cr). San José, Costa Rica. February 13.

Niemi, Richard G., and Laura Winsky. 1987. "Membership Turnover in State Legislatures: Trends and Effects of Districting." *Legislative Studies Quarterly* 12:115–23.

Norrander, Barbara, and Clyde Wilcox. 1998. "The Geography of Gender Power: Women in State Legislatures." In *Women and Elective Office: Past, Present, and Future,* ed. Sue Thomas and Clyde Wilcox. New York: Oxford University Press.

Novak, Robert D. 1993. "Term Limits, In Trenton . . . ." *Washington Post,* June 24, A19.

Opheim, Cynthia. 1994. "The Effect of U.S. State Legislative Term Limits Revisited." *Legislative Studies Quarterly* 19.49–59.

Petracca, Mark P. 1991. *The Poison of Professional Politics.* Policy analysis 151. Washington, DC: Cato Institute.

Petracca, Mark P. 1992a. "A Legislature in Transition: The California Experience with Term Limits." Paper presented at the American Political Science Association annual meeting, Washington, DC.

Petracca, Mark P. 1992b. "Rotation in Office: The History of an Idea." In *Limiting Legislative Terms,* ed. Gerald Benjamin and Michael J. Malbin. Washington, DC: Congressional Quarterly Press.

Petracca, Mark P. 1998. "California's Experience with Legislative Term Limits." *Term Limits Outlook Series,* (April): 1–48.

Polsby, Nelson W. 1968. "The Institutionalization of the House of Representatives." *American Political Science Review* 62:144–68.

Polsby, Nelson W. 1991. "Some Arguments against Congressional Term Limitations." *Harvard Journal of Law and Public Policy* 16:1516–26.

Pound, William. 1992. "State Legislative Careers: Twenty-Five Years of Reform." In *Changing Patterns in State Legislative Careers,* ed. Gary F. Moncrief and Joel A. Thompson. Ann Arbor: University of Michigan Press.

Powell, Lynda. 1993. "Electoral Competition in House Primary Elections." Paper presented at the American Political Science Association annual meeting, Washington, DC.

Rohde, David W. 1991. *Parties and Leaders in the Postreform House.* Chicago: University of Chicago Press.

Rosenthal, Alan. 1992. "The Effects of Term Limits on Legislatures: A Comment." In *Limiting Legislative Terms,* ed. Gerald Benjamin and Michael J. Malbin. Washington, DC: Congressional Quarterly Press.

Schlesinger, Joseph A. 1966. *Ambition and Politics: Political Careers in the United States.* Chicago: Rand McNally.

Schlesinger, Joseph A. 1991. *Political Parties and the Winning of Office.* Ann Arbor: University of Michigan Press.

Schrag, Peter. 1995. "The Populist Road to Hell." *American Prospect* 24:24–30.

Squire, Peverill. 1988. "Career Opportunities and Membership Stability in Legislatures." *Legislative Studies Quarterly* 13:65–82.

Squire, Peverill. 1992a. "Changing State Legislative Leadership Careers." In *Changing Patterns in State Legislative Careers,* ed. Gary F. Moncrief and Joel A. Thompson. Ann Arbor: University of Michigan Press.

Squire, Peverill. 1992b. "Legislative Professionalization and Membership Diversity in State Legislatures." *Legislative Studies Quarterly* 17:69–79.

Squire, Peverill. 1993. "Professionalization and Public Opinion of State Legislatures." *Journal of Politics* 55:479–91.

Stanley, Harold W., and Richard G. Niemi. 1998. *Vital Statistics on American Politics, 1997–1998.* Washington, DC: Congressional Quarterly Press.

Thomas, Sue. 1998. "Women and Elective Office: Past, Present, and Future." In *Women and Elective Office: Past, Present, and Future,* ed. Sue Thomas and Clyde Wilcox. New York: Oxford University Press.

U.S. Department of Commerce. Various years. *State Government Finances.* Washington, DC: U.S. Department of Commerce.

Weber, Ronald E., Harvey J. Tucker, and Paul Brace. 1991. "Vanishing Marginals in State Legislative Elections." *Legislative Studies Quarterly* 16:29–47.

Weberg, Brian, and Beth Bazar. 1988. *Legislative Staff Services: 50 State Profiles.* Denver: National Conference of State Legislators.

Weldon, Jeffrey. 1994. "No Reelection and the Mexican Congress." Ph.D. diss., University of California, San Diego.

Will, George F. 1992. *Restoration: Congress, Term Limits, and the Recovery of Deliberative Democracy.* New York: Free Press.

Zupan, M. A. 1990. "The Last Period Problem in Politics: Do Congressional Representatives Not Subject to a Reelection Constraint Alter Their Voting Behavior?" *Public Choice* 65:167–80.

Author Index

Subject Index